THE CHURCH IN HER HOUSE

THE CHURCH IN HER HOUSE
A Feminist Emancipatory Prayer Book for Christian Communities

MARJORIE PROCTER-SMITH

THE PILGRIM PRESS

CLEVELAND

In loving memory of MARTHA GILMORE

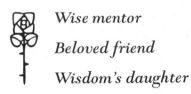

Wise mentor

Beloved friend

Wisdom's daughter

The Pilgrim Press, 700 Prospect Avenue, Cleveland, Ohio 44115–1100
thepilgrimpress.com

© 2008 Marjorie Procter-Smith

Scripture quotations, unless otherwise noted, are from the New Revised Standard
Version of the Bible, © 1989 by the Division of Christian Education of the National
Council of Churches of Christ in the United States of America, and are used by
permission. Changes have been made for inclusivity.

All rights reserved. Published 2008

The author gratefully acknowledges permission to reprint the following:
Filipe Tohi, "Christ the Anchor," in *Christ for All People: Celebrating a World
of Christian Art*, ed. Ron O'Grady (Maryknoll, N.Y.: Orbis Press, 2001).
Used by permission.

"A Meal Prayer of Bitterness," adapted from *Praying with Our Eyes Open:
Engendering Feminist Liturgical Prayer* by Marjorie Procter-Smith © 1995 by
Abingdon Press, 1995. Adapted by permission.

Printed in the United States of America on acid-free paper that contains
post-consumer fiber.

13   12   11   10   09   08   5   4   3   2   1

Library of Congress Cataloging-in-Publication Data

Procter-Smith, Marjorie.
    The church in her house : creating emancipatory feminist liturgies for
Christian communities / Marjorie Procter-Smith.
        p. cm.
    ISBN–13: 978–0–8298–1701–0 (alk. paper)
    1. Feminist theology.   2. Liturgics.   I. Title.
BT83.55.P75 2007
264.0082—dc22   2007040165

CONTENTS

USING THIS BOOK

The Church in Her House: A Feminist Emancipatory Prayer Book for Christian Communities is intended for Christian communities and individuals seeking liturgies and prayers that foster freedom, justice, and radical democracy. The title expresses and invokes many dimensions of such a praying community, and authorizes the claiming of liberating gathering space.

The phrase "the church in her house" is taken, first of all, from the historically contested Christian Testament references to house churches led by women. For some of these women we have names: Nympha in Laodecia (Col. 4:15); Prisca in Asia (1 Cor. 16:19 and Rom. 16:3–5); Lydia of Thyatira (Acts 16:11–15), and Mary the mother of John Mark (Acts 12:12). These women and their sisters whose names have been forgotten stand in the same company with Jewish women of the time who were leaders of synagogues. Recovery of ancient inscriptions and epitaphs gives us the names of some of these Jewish religious leaders: Rufina, Sophia, Sara, Beronika, Mannine, Faustina, Rebeka, Eulgia, Makaria. On the basis of the considerable evidence, it is clear that there were many worshiping communities in early Christianity and in contemporary Judaism that were led by women. On the other hand, the early attempt to suppress or diminish the importance of these women leaders is also amply evident in "corrections" of women's names into men's names, in suppression of actual names, and in attempts to reinterpret the role of women leaders as ancillary or secondary to men. As early Christians and their Jewish contemporaries gathered for worship and study in assemblies led by women and in women's space, so also women today can lay claim to authority and leadership. At the same time, progressive communities and individuals who wish to claim the center of Christian identity frequently find themselves marginalized and their claims to Christian identity rejected by regressive and repressive individuals, communities, and organizations. By invoking early Christian communities meeting in a woman's house, this prayer book claims the historical precedent of these ancient communities that resisted the oppressive orderings of the religious, social, and political world in which they lived, and that created an emancipatory alternative space "in her house."

The phrase "in her house" also evokes another biblical house: that of Wisdom.

Wisdom has built her house,
    she has hewn her seven pillars.
She has slaughtered her animals, she has mixed her wine,
    she has also set her table.
She has sent out her women ministers, she calls
    from the highest places in the town . . .
"Come, eat of my bread
    and drink of the wine I have mixed. . . ." (Prov. 9:1–5)

Wisdom, the deep understanding that comes from living fully, is the aim of every religion. Deeper than mere knowledge, it is that radically democratic insight that is readily available to anyone. Although it is often found among those who have lived long, it is also often delightfully present in the very young. Sometimes highly educated persons possess wisdom, but it is also as likely to be found among those to whom formal education has been denied or limited. In the biblical books of Proverbs and Wisdom, this attribute is presented as an essential aspect of the Holy One and is personified as a woman. Divine Wisdom is presented as a friend to human beings who eagerly seeks us and offers us her gifts of truth, insight, discretion, and justice. In her tireless pursuit of human beings, she sets her table and opens her house to all who wish to find wisdom. This open, welcoming, seven-pillared house is the liberating space envisioned in this prayer book for communities in our day who seek to enter her house and learn from her.

The phrase "in her house" reminds us of the house of another woman or women: the home of Mary and Martha of Bethany, who opened their house to the friend of human beings, Jesus. Theirs was a house of hospitality.

Not for Women Only, but Sometimes

Wisdom's house, the church in her house, the house of Mary and Martha of Bethany: all of these are open houses, welcoming all in radical equality. Persons seeking to live in the world and with one another in this community of equals are invited in and welcomed. And all persons seeking a community of equals can be confident that their particular spiritual and ritual needs will be honored.

At times, radical equality demands that space be given and honored for groups within the community of radical equality to gather as distinct groups. This means that women, marginalized and silenced in mainstream churches, can identify their needs for particular gatherings, such as, perhaps, celebrations of first menstruation for girls or menopause for women. This also means that gay and lesbian and transgendered people can identify their needs for particular gatherings. And that African Americans can identify their needs for particular gatherings, and Native Americans theirs, and Latinos and Latinas theirs, and persons with disabilities theirs, too.

These and other gatherings to attend to particular spiritual and ritual needs not only honor the needs of members of the community, but also recognize the intersecting and overlapping forms of oppression experienced by members of the community. This overlapping and interlocking structure of oppression has been named "kyriarchy" by Elisabeth Schüssler Fiorenza. This term, meaning literally "rule of the masters," points out that the more familiar term "patriarchy" suggests that men (literally, "fathers") are rulers. But as men of color, or male slaves, or men who are gay, or men who are disabled, could attest, this is a limited understanding. Only by making room to name, address, and respond to the needs and interests generated by these multiple oppressions can we create communities of radical and meaningful equality. Only by recognizing the ways in which our differing oppressions work together to sustain and support social, political, and religious patriarchal structures can we begin to claim common ground and work together across gender, racial, and ethnic lines. This common work we are calling feminist emancipatory work. By "feminist" I mean to place women at the center, to make women visible, audible, and active. By "emancipatory" I mean being oriented toward the freedom of *all* people, recognizing the intersection and interrelationship of these multiple forms of oppression.

Using This Book

When I need to create a liturgy for a particular occasion, I find that most often I draw materials and ideas from many sources, making each liturgy a kind of patchwork in which each individual piece is beautiful on its own, but these pieces taken together make an even more beautiful whole. Like a patchwork quilt, the liturgical elements (prayers, movements and gestures, rituals, and symbols) are often taken out of their original context and repurposed for this unique event.

Like a patchwork quilt, too, a liturgical event must have an overall shape to it, to give it movement and purpose and beauty. Having a basic understanding of some of the shapes common to Christian worship and human rituals can help you make your own "patchwork quilt" liturgies for the events in your life and the life of your community.

Unlike many prayer books and denominational worship books, this book contains almost no complete worship services. I find that such services rarely serve exactly as printed. Instead of a prayer book to be used in liturgical services, this is a workbook, a resource, and a guide. Use it to plan and design Christian feminist liturgies for your women's group, for your Bible study group, for your ecumenical women's gathering, for your congregation, for your community, for your own personal prayer life. Carry it with you on the bus; mark in it; borrow, adapt, or rewrite its prayers and liturgies; use it up. If it offers you inspiration, insight, resources, discussion, food for reflection and prayer, it has fulfilled its purpose.

Each chapter is arranged in five sections. The first section, "Thinking about . . . ," includes a summary of the theological issues, the practical issues, and the process for generating a liturgy. Read this section if you are curious about the background of the liturgical materials in the section or the basic concepts that inform them. Having some basic information can help you create liturgies and prayers that are fitted to your situation and needs.

The second section, "Spiritual Disciplines for . . . ," suggests one or more spiritual practices that can foster a deeper understanding of the topic of the chapter. Typically, these are disciplines that can be undertaken by an individual, a community or subgroup of a community, or all of these. The creation of liturgies and prayers can itself be a spiritual discipline. The suggestions in this section provide foundational work for preparing to undertake the liturgical work of making prayer happen for oneself and for others.

The section entitled "Shapes for . . ." provides some basic patterns for the liturgies included in that chapter. These patterns may serve as templates for your own prayers and liturgies and provide tools for planning teams.

The section "Prayers for . . ." offers prayers and liturgies or parts of liturgies for the events of each chapter. You may decide to use these prayers and liturgies just as they are. But if you print a bulletin or order of service that includes these texts, please include a credit line: "From Marjorie Procter-Smith, *The Church in Her House: A Feminist Emancipatory Prayer Book for Christian Communities* (Cleveland: Pilgrim Press, 2008)." Or you may want to adapt or even rewrite them completely to speak to your occasion, event, community, or personal need. Or you may find that they work better as idea starters, as inspiration for writing your own prayers and liturgies in your own voice in ways that express the life of your own community. Use them freely as seems best, and be creative!

And finally, each chapter includes the section "Resources for . . . ," providing additional references for suitable prayers and liturgies for these events or just for further reading. Here you will find other collections of liturgies and prayers that can be stitched in to your own liturgies. These are some of the resources that I have found to be helpful for me in thinking about and designing liturgies. I hope you will use these lists as a springboard to discovering your own favorite resources, and that you will add to these lists. As in the case of the prayers and liturgies in this book, though, be courteous and respectful of the work of others, and follow copyright guidelines scrupulously. Always give credit where it is due and, if necessary, ask permission before printing any published prayers, liturgies, or music (either words or music). An excellent resource for discovering how to do this is Church Music Publishers Association. The website, http://www.cmpamusic.org/html/main.isx?sub=5, provides basic copyright information and help finding out how to secure permissions for use of published materials.

Thus it is not necessary or even particularly desirable to read this book of liturgies straight through. Instead, it is best to use it as a ready resource for your own prayer life, for that of your community, or for the planning of a special or occasional event in your Christian life.

ONE

PATHWAYS AND SIGNPOSTS

I am about to do a new thing;
now it springs forth, do you not perceive it?
I will make a way in the wilderness
and rivers in the desert.

—Isaiah 43:19

THINKING ABOUT CHRISTIAN FEMINIST RITUAL

The work of feminist liturgy is to make new pathways through the largely uncharted territory of liturgy that places at its center the lives and hopes and desires of women and other marginalized and rejected and forgotten communities. This work begins with but is not limited to the pathway of women's experience. It is essential to begin here because of the history of exclusion and the harm done by this history of exclusion.

Feminist Ritual Pathways

Women as a class have been systematically excluded from leadership of and, under certain circumstances, even participation in Christian liturgies. The rejection of women as ordained or officially recognized and authorized ritual leaders is well known and continues today in many Christian communities. What is less well known is the history of denial of access to communion or other Christian worship gatherings because of imagined uncleanness of women who are menstruating or who have recently given birth. Women have not only been forbidden to speak or read or preach or preside in public worship, they also have been forbidden to sing. Women have been denied the power to make symbols and create liturgies. Women have been excluded from the central symbols and stories that form the foundation of Christian liturgies and prayers. The stories told, the stories that provide the storehouse of images and symbols reflected in Christian worship, overwhelmingly present men as central actors, men's interests and concerns as central concerns, men's lives as normative. Liturgical symbols and language, starting with language about God, are almost without exception male-centered.

The harm done by this history of exclusion is widespread. Not only does it marginalize women and women's interests, experiences, desires, and needs; it also harms the church as a whole. It denies the church both the challenge and the blessing of these interests, experiences, desires, and needs, and the church is the poorer for it. The church's liturgies are impoverished when women's voices are silenced, women's stories are omitted, women's experiences are distorted or rejected. Any corrective liturgical work must recognize the loss and harm as well as the blessings and challenges.

A progressive Christian community must take as its central work this corrective activity, developing and engaging in a process of reinterpretation and reimagining of culture, religion, and ritual. And it must take it unapologetically, recognizing the multiple forms that kyriarchal oppression takes and the myriad ways that oppression of women as a group intersects with and reinforces the oppression of others. This means making a way through the wilderness of the church's historic rejection and demonization of women, naming and confronting the harm done, and saying "no" to those practices and beliefs that continue the history of harm. This also means making a way through the desert of silence and erasure of women's lives and stories, seeking and finding streams of life-giving water that can nourish and refresh the church.

In order to make our feminist emancipatory way through the wilderness we will need tools for breaking a trail and we'll need supplies to sustain us on the way. We will need the sharpest feminist interpretive tools available:

1. The sharp blade of *suspicion* cuts through the undergrowth to ask, Is this the whole story? The tool of interpretive suspicion asks, Who benefits from this interpretation or this practice, and who suffers? What has been distorted, hidden, and left out? What needs to be removed, for the well-being of all who would travel this pathway? What has been allowed to grow and flourish that is in fact toxic and that needs to be cut out and removed? Once the weeds and rank growth of kyriarchal practice have been cut back, we can take up the next tool.

2. The spade of *retrieval* will allow us to identify and recover the small and tender shoots of hidden and forgotten practices and stories, to dig them out and to graft them onto the roots of the tradition's practices, to strengthen and nurture life-enhancing growth along the path.

3. The final tool is one that permits us to smooth and widen the path, to make it as fully accessible as possible. The tool of *affirmation* is one that confirms us in our trek through the wilderness

and that encourages and strengthens and welcomes us into spaces formerly forbidden to us. This tool broadens our access to the path, confirms our right to be here, and makes the way smooth.

When we find our way onto the path, we discover that we already carry with us resources for the journey. We have at hand the lived wisdom of our lives, our bodies, our suffering and struggles, and our relationships.

The wisdom of our lives

First, we know that our experience is socially constructed by patriarchal definitions of what constitutes human experience. Patriarchal definitions of "human experience" take the dominant white, upperclass, straight, able-bodied male as the normative human. Human experiences that fail to fit into this norm are defined as deviant, abnormal, or otherwise marginal. But when we delve deeper into what we know to be true about our own lives, and when we can set aside the constant messages about who fails to fit into the dominant story about what human experience is supposed to be (and this is hard and constant work indeed), then we begin to be able to name our own experience, to claim our own knowledge as real and true. And this knowledge—which we must always be seeking, learning to listen deeply to our own selves and learning to "hear one another into speech," in the words of Nelle Morton[1]—this knowledge offers us the sustenance we need to travel the path into feminist emancipatory community.

What we hear when we listen to our deepest selves, what we hear when we listen deeply to one another, is the practical experience of lived oppression. We know what it is to be defined as other, as inferior, as defective, as outsider. And this knowledge serves to ground us in reality and in truth. It reminds us of all that we have learned not only about ourselves, but about the kyriarchal world in which we all live. We know this world from our unique perspective, not as those who receive all benefits from this world, but as those who at times suffer from its inequities. And our experience grants us empathy, if we choose to exercise it, with those who suffer differently from the same kyriarchal oppression. The pathway of empathy makes it possible for us to form community with those whose experience differs from ours but whose hearts long for a world in which such suffering and oppression no longer occur.

What we hear when we listen to our deep selves and when we truly hear one another is our own practical religious experience. We know, however dimly sometimes, that we experience the Holy in our own way, and that we experience the Holy in our daily and ordinary lives. This experience of the Holy requires no mediation of authorities or patriarchs. It is woven through our lives, in our relationships with others, with the world around us, both animate and inanimate, in the miraculous workings of our fragile bodies, in our struggles to do good and to live well, in our deepest longings for peace, for joy, for connection. At times, under duress or threat, we have hidden this experience of the Holy from the eyes and ears of others, who might reject, judge, or deny our experience. And at times we have hidden this experience even from ourselves. Yet, at the same time, we know that we long for a time and a place that makes room for our experiences of the Holy, a time and place that recognizes and celebrates those experiences. It is that knowledge, that longing, that "dreaming of a place not like this one," in the words of Anne Cameron,[2] that motivates our working and praying for change. It is the aim of this book to foster the full recognition and celebration of this knowledge, to enable us to live fully in our own appropriation of the Holy and to share that experience with others.

The wisdom of our bodies

A second important pathway to feminist emancipatory community, as well as a source of our experience and of the experience of women, is our bodies. Christianity taken as a whole has an ambivalent attitude regarding human bodies in general. On the one hand, the doctrine of the incarnation—classical Christianity's firm insistence that Jesus was fully human and that God took on human flesh in Jesus—sets a strong foundation for a positive assessment of the blessedness of the human body. On the other hand, a collusion of philosophical dualism (including gender dualism), cultural notions of purity and contamination, and (mis)interpretation of creation stories produced a strong tradition within Christianity that rejected the flesh as evil, saw human bodies as barriers to spiritual growth, and identified women especially with the sins of the flesh, especially sexuality. So we all bear the weight of this tradition of disapproval of our bodies by our faith, but for those of us with women's bodies, the weight is especially heavy. Women's bodies and their imagined dangers, pollutions, and temptations have provided the primary reason for barring women from exercising liturgical and ecclesial authority. Progressive Christian communities must confront this painful legacy, discover the ways in which it has hampered all of us, women and men, and see the myriad ways in which it influences the church's response not only to women's leadership, but also to understandings of race, class, sexual orientation, and physical ability.

As we come to a deeper understanding of the significance of this double heritage, we also come to a deeper appreciation of the incarnational tradition of our faith and the power of affirming our God-given bodies in all their diversity, beauty, and fragility. A major challenge for Christian feminist communities is discovering authentic, powerful, and empowering images of human bodies, especially of female human bodies. Our religious images of women tend to emphasize women either as dangerous sexual beings or as submissive and docile maidens or mothers. Recovering and constructing positive, powerful, and authentic images of women, in visual and three-dimensional art as well as in verbal imagery, is a major ongoing task of feminist communities.

This task requires understanding women's bodily experiences as a significant source of wisdom. This process of understanding and interpretation typically begins with giving positive attention to the natural cycles of women's bodies: menarche, menstruation, menopause, pregnancy, childbirth, and lactation. The wisdom of our bodies' cycles offers important ways of understanding ourselves as human creatures in harmony with other living creatures. The beginning and ending of these natural cycles can link us with other natural cycles of the earth, especially with the growing and waning light of the sun and of the moon. Rituals and symbols that affirm and respect the wisdom of the cycles of women's bodies can bless these cycles for women who experience them, but also for men who participate in them through the natural cycles of the earth. Feminist emancipatory communities can develop rituals for individual and community use that celebrate menarche, menstruation, and menopause, pregnancy, childbirth, and lactation. Similarly, rituals and prayers that celebrate and honor the wisdom of old age, in both men and women, reclaim the gifts of crones and elders that are often rejected in the larger society. It is especially important for children and youth to participate in these celebrations, as they can shape relationships with senior adults and form young people to grow into spiritual maturity as they age.

The wisdom of suffering and struggle

To live is to know suffering. To struggle against suffering, to resist suffering, is to claim one's life as one's own. Since all we have in this world is our life, the emancipatory community claims and values resistance to suffering, especially the suffering of women. In all places, in all times, women and other oppressed people have struggled against their own oppression, in ways both small and great. From these struggles we learn, and to these struggles we give honor in our rituals and in our lives. We remember, first, the many ways that people have resisted and continue to resist their own oppression and suffering. We stand with those who suffer and struggle to own their own lives, and we struggle to own our own lives as well. In the process of resisting suffering and standing with those who also resist, we claim the power to name the evil that causes suffering. In naming evil, we call to account those responsible, and we refuse evil's continued cost. Ritually, this may take the form of curses or laments, naming suffering from which there is no resolution, and calling to account those we hold responsible, including, at times, the Holy One. But cursing and lament, as expressions of righteous anger and grief, also call for healing of harm done. Rituals of healing and blessing are also needed to move those who suffer from the helplessness of loss to the hope of well-being. Those who have suffered sexual and domestic violence and abuse have much to teach us who have been fortunate: about struggle, about evil, about resistance and recovery, about cursing and blessing.

The wisdom of relationships

The life lived in connection is a life of fullness and blessing. Women's connections with other women form the basis for celebrating and lamenting our common ground as well as honoring our differences of race, of class, of sexual preference, of ability, and of myriad other differences we discover when we share common life. This honest connection makes it possible for us to stand with one another in our different struggles and sufferings and hopes, as well as to hold one another accountable to the hope of our faith. As well, we claim our relationships with men, seeing our common and shared lives as a blessing and daring to be honest with one another about our differences. Finally, we claim our connections with the nonhuman world, especially the interrelationship we enjoy with other species and indeed with the life of the planet itself.

Learning the wisdom, through ritual and prayer and through daily living, to travel this pathway requires patient and prayerful discernment, as well as courage and determination. And as we learn the wisdom of women's lives and struggles and hopes, we learn of all those who seek to own their own lives and to share community with us.

Christian Signposts

As we are marking out our own feminist ritual pathways, seeking the faint traces of those who have gone before us, using the sharp tools of feminist insight and wisdom to make our way through the wilderness of kyriarchy, we are also seeking Christian signposts along the way. As Christians seeking emancipatory community, we look for the signs of our faith, the markers that show us to be part of the Christian movement that celebrates life and community, that is willing to dwell in Wisdom's welcoming house. We seek signs that Christianity has room for us, that it contains within it feminist emancipatory moments and seeds of change.

These Christian signposts mark out the shape and direction of the faith. They are not idols in themselves, but they point beyond themselves to the reality that shapes our lives. In the broadest possible terms, these signposts give shape to this prayer book and help emancipatory Christian communities identify with the Christian tradition.

What are these signposts? They are the simple, human things: meals, washing, communication with others. Traditionally, these have been called Holy Communion, baptism, and prayer. They are the marks of our identity, our family album and our family stories—the Bible, our history, and especially our hidden and forgotten stories. They are the personal signposts that measure the turning points in our lives—partnering, birth and death, transitions into new stages of our lives: marriages, funerals, adulthood, and old age rites. All of these things, and more, Christians have been doing for centuries upon centuries.

When we find our way on feminist pathways to Wisdom's house, we reimagine and celebrate these Christian signposts, these Christian meals, washings, communication, and stories in ways that place at the center those of us who have been placed at the margins by the kyriarchal structures and stories and practices. This process has two steps. The first is a recognition and recovery of what is most fundamental about these Christian signposts: the animal necessity of washing, eating, communing; the human necessity of storytelling and remembering and marking life transitions and changes. When we look deeply, beneath the centuries of kyriarchal claiming of authority over these actions and practices, we see that no special words, actions, or leaders are necessary; that the only restrictions we need place on these practices have to do with our individual and shared well-being. Baptism is washing. Eucharist or Lord's Supper or Holy Communion is eating. Prayer is communicating. Scripture and preaching are telling stories and remembering. And all human beings know how to do these things. So we begin by asking: How can the washing of baptism make clear the simple human act that it is, free of kyriarchal restrictions? How can the meal of the Eucharist clearly express the simple human act of eating and drinking together? How can the work of prayer take on the simple human action of communicating? How can scripture and preaching be made into our stories, told and remembered and celebrated and mourned? In this way, we claim the common human experience that connects us with one another and with all people.

The second step is to claim the Christian meaning of these human actions, their connection with the Christian story (which we also claim as our story), and our place in the center of that story and those actions. We claim washing as entering into the Christian community as Wisdom's house, as the church in her house. We claim Eucharist as the meal shared in the presence of Wisdom, with women at the table, the sharing of food being an act of open-hearted hospitality. We claim scripture as the hidden stories of our lives, read between the lines of the kyriarchal canon, given life from forgotten tales, brought from the margin of the page to the center of the story. We claim the turnings and changes of our lives as the stuff of seasonal celebrations of life and of change, told and told again in remembrance of those who have gone before us, including Jesus, in whose memory we celebrate all this, and in whose footsteps we follow along the pathways to Wisdom's house, to the church in her house.

A SPIRITUAL DISCIPLINE
OF FEMINIST DISCERNMENT

We women have been systematically deprived of our voices and our sense of moral authority. We have been silenced, ignored, rejected, ridiculed, and dismissed as moral agents. This is also true for any enslaved groups, persons of despised status, children, and nonhuman creatures of all kinds. When one stops and thinks about it, it is only a very tiny percentage of beings whose voices have been recognized, authorized, and empowered to speak. Feminist emancipatory discernment requires, first of all, that we discover our authentic voices and claim our power to make good decisions for ourselves and for the common good.

Such a recovery is a lifelong process, in which one is continually learning to hear oneself into speech, to learn the voice of one's own heart, and, to echo Ntozake Shange, "to find god in ourselves, and to love her fiercely."[3] Taking the big picture, one could say that all of the spiritual disciplines, liturgical practices, and shared emancipatory community are means of enabling this process. But in the short run, here are some suggestions to foster a strong sense of voice and trust in one's own ability to make good decisions.

1. *Keep a journal.* There are many different models for journaling, ranging from the highly structured to the more informal and spontaneous, from the private journaling read only by oneself to shared reading in a small group of trusted friends. Not all methods are good for everyone. Experiment until you find or create a method that works for you. But whatever method you choose, be as honest as you can be in the writing of it, and reread it often. This will help you see what voice is inside you and how you are making decisions and living with them.

2. *Find a spiritual companion.* A trusted friend who can be honest with you, and you with her, can be invaluable in hearing one another into speech. As with journaling, honesty is essential.

3. *Read memoirs and autobiographies of people whose voices have been suppressed.* By reading their own words about their coming to

find their own words you can put your own process into a larger context. It is sometimes easy to imagine that no one else has been where we are. It is good to meet, through literature, others who have been where we are—and have found a way out.

4. *Read literature and poetry.* Both literary fiction and poetry invite us in to another world in which we both experience the world of another unlike us and find ourselves. Reading good stories can help us learn to hear and tell our own stories better.

5. *Practice telling your truth when you can.* Every day, make a decision to tell your truth at least once.

PATTERNS OF FEMINIST PATHWAYS

The process of discerning the feminist pathway marked by Christian signposts is, first of all, a communal process. While personal prayer, contemplation, study, and reflection are essential to this process, it is necessary to test one's discernment against the discernments of others who are on the pathway with us. This is not an uncritical process. The exercise of judgment and the development of a feminist capacity to discern the way and make sound judgments about that pathway are themselves part of a lifetime process.

One of the most significant judgments that must be made is the one some feminists have named deciding whether to be "on or off the bus." This is a way of speaking about the often difficult relationships feminists and other progressive Christians have with established church institutions. As the metaphor suggests, this is less a judgment about the proper pathway than it is a judgment about the best means of transportation along that pathway. Is the institutional church ("the bus") the best way to get to Wisdom's house? Or is an alternative means of transportation better for our spiritual well-being? And of course the question of the bus's destination is very much to the point. Is this institutional bus actually going to the church in her house? For many feminists and others marginalized and rejected by institutional Christianity, the bus is not the best way to get where we are going, nor are we sure that we have the same destination in mind. Getting "off the bus," and perhaps into some other religious or spiritual community, or none, may indeed be the best judgment for some. For these, the choice may be painful, or it may be a relief. For others, the bus of the institutional church, for all its sins and pain inflicted, remains the best way of navigating the feminist pathway or at least of keeping us mindful of the Christian signposts that we desire to mark our way forward. For some of us who still ride the bus, the decision to do so may be a daily decision, subject to review and further discernment.

It is within this larger context of feminist discernment that liturgical and ritual judgments take place. And in their turn, they too demand discernment, from the decision to hold a liturgy for some purpose, through the planning and design process, to the letting go of the liturgy into its life as a living prayer of an individual or a community. This process is considered more fully in the next chapter, "Patterns."

Here are some suggestions for developing individual and communal practices of feminist Christian discernment.

1. *Begin with prayer and silence.* Whether seeking individual or communal discernment, placing the process in a context of prayer and contemplation, with their qualities of attentive listening, is an important beginning.

2. *Name the matter on which discernment is sought.* Often the process of naming the question or issue suggests possible answers or solutions, or at least greater clarity. If this is a matter for individual discernment, putting the naming in writing can be helpful. It can also be helpful, even if this is an individual matter, to talk with a trusted confidant about it, someone who can listen carefully and provide clear and nonjudgmental feedback. If it is a communal matter, the first step is to agree upon what the problem or question is. This step can take more time and patience and mutual listening than one might think.

3. *Generate many possible solutions or answers.* It is important not to limit the imagination at this point in the process to open oneself or one's community to new possibilities. Set aside for the moment possible objections or disagreements (either internally or communally) to let the Spirit move. Listen carefully to the ideas and suggestions that come. Take notes.

4. *Pause for prayer and silence.* Allow time for the ideas that have come forth to settle in the mind and heart. Pay careful attention to the ideas to which you are most drawn, and to the ideas to which you are least attracted. Consider what it is that attracts or repels you, and ask yourself why. Give yourself or the community plenty of time in this step. It may be useful to wait upon the process overnight. Sleep—and the simple passage of time—often provides insight and perspective.

5. *Discuss the ideas.* Use a process of mutual invitation as developed by Eric Law or a Quaker method of consensus building to foster

open and trusting conversation in a communal process. Remember to include and listen to wisdom from all, as in Wisdom's house. When useful, include breaks for silence. If this is an individual process, this is another moment when it would be valuable to consult with a trusted friend.

6. *Make use of feminist emancipatory criteria.* Who benefits from one solution or another? Who suffers? Where are the women? The children? Others who have been marginalized and silenced? Are they present? Are their voices heard? What about the voiceless: those who are far away, those who are absent, the members of the community of the earth and the environment? Who speaks for their interests? Depending on the nature of the decision, in a communal discernment process it may be valuable to designate someone to speak for the voiceless in the discussion.

7. *Make room for dissent.* The power to say "no" is essential if one's "yes" is to have meaning. Resist the temptation to suppress disagreement and dissent. Sometimes the greatest wisdom and work of the Spirit can be found in voices of dissent.

8. *Listen for consensus.* If this is an individual process, you may become aware of a strong leading in one direction. Pay attention to this leading, but listen for any internal dissent as well. In a communal context, the community will notice when consensus begins to emerge in the discussion. If this is the case, it is helpful to begin to attempt to name the consensus. This may also take some time.

9. *Close in prayer and silence.* When consensus (internal or communal) is reached, close the session in prayer, spoken or silent.

PRAYERS FOR FEMINIST PATHWAYS

A PRAYER FOR DISCERNMENT

Open our eyes, open our minds, open our hearts.
Show the way, drive us out of the cramped and silent spaces,
lead us into the open and unmarked path
for your name's sake.

With your strong Spirit's urging,
with the fire and cloud of your presence before us,
with the song of Miriam ringing in our ears,
push us into your freedom.

For your name's sake,
Liberator,
Savior,
Guide.

THANKSGIVING FOR CONSENSUS FOUND

For what we have heard,
we thank you.
For what we have found,
we give you praise.
For what we have missed,
we ask enlightenment.
For what we still seek,
we ask your leading.
And in all things,
we give you thanks.

RESOURCES FOR CHRISTIAN FEMINIST PATHWAYS

Berger, Teresa. *Dissident Daughters: Feminist Liturgies in Global Context.* Louisville: Westminster John Knox Press, 2002.

_____. *Women's Ways of Worship: Gender Analysis and Liturgical History.* Collegeville, Minn.: Liturgical Press, 1999.

Dougherty, Rose Mary. *Group Spiritual Direction: Community for Discernment.* Mahwah, N.J.: Paulist Press, 1995.

Elkins, Heather Murray. *Worshiping Women: Re-Forming God's People for Praise.* Nashville: Abingdon Press, 1994.

Flinders, Carol Lee. *At the Root of This Longing: Reconciling a Spiritual Hunger and a Feminist Thirst.* San Francisco: HarperCollins, 1998.

Gallagher, Nora. *Practicing Resurrection: A Memoir of Discernment.* New York: Alfred A. Knopf, 2003.

Law, Eric H. F. *The Wolf Shall Dwell with the Lamb: A Spirituality for Leadership in a Multicultural Community.* St. Louis, Mo.: Chalice Press, 1993.

Procter-Smith, Marjorie. *In Her Own Rite: Constructing Feminist Liturgical Tradition.* Akron, Ohio: OSL Publication, 2000.

_____. *Praying with Our Eyes Open: Engendering Feminist Liturgical Prayer.* Nashville: Abingdon Press, 1995.

Procter-Smith, Marjorie, and Janet R. Walton, eds. *Women at Worship: Interpretations of North American Diversity.* Louisville: Westminster John Knox Press, 1993.

Schüssler Fiorenza, Elisabeth. *Wisdom's Ways: Introducing Feminist Biblical Interpretation.* Maryknoll, N.Y.: Orbis Press, 2001.

Walton, Janet R. *Feminist Liturgy: A Matter of Justice.* Collegeville, Minn.: Liturgical Press, 2000.

TWO

PATTERNS

So then, friends, we are children, not of the slave
but of the free woman.
For freedom Christ has set us free.
Stand firm, therefore, and do not submit to a yoke of slavery.

— Galations 4:31–5:1

THINKING ABOUT RITUAL PATTERNS

Human beings seem to be, by nature, ritualizing animals. In fact, ritualizing behavior is something we humans share with other animals. But as humans, we tend to want to assign meanings to our ritualizing and, in turn, to ritualize events that are full of meaning for us. Human ritualizing is patterned behavior, and understanding these patterns and some of the principles that lie behind them can make it easier to generate rituals that can do what we need our rituals to do.

All rituals are invented

Where do our religious rituals come from? How does one go about creating a ritual? Is it even possible to create meaningful religious rituals ourselves? Some ritual theorists have argued that ritual creation is impossible, that rituals (and symbols) must arise from the subconscious, the collective unconscious, or some other source outside ourselves that is ultimately uncontrollable. They argue that symbols and rituals are born, not made, so to speak. This assumption reinforces the notion that ritual is an essentially conservative activity, intended to maintain the status quo, either by resolving conflict or by renewing common beliefs and practices by means of invoking superhuman or divine powers.

However, another school of thought, represented by the generative ritual practices of feminist liturgical groups, sees both the possibility of ritual creation and the transformative potential of ritual. More to the point, perhaps, we all create rituals all the time in our daily lives: the small rituals of rising in the morning and retiring at night and the larger rituals commemorating significant events in our lives. The parent who plans a child's birthday celebration, the coworkers who host a retirement party, the friends who gather to be with a grieving widow—all are creating rituals. Rituals are in fact ways in which we construct our lives and give meaning and order to events both large and small. They are the strategies by which we navigate our way through the day and through our lives.

At the same time, we often take for granted the more formal religious rituals of our lives as if they were givens: baptisms, marriages, funerals, regular occasions of worship, both daily and weekly, and religious festivals of various kinds. These religious events often appear to us as if they were indeed arising from someplace beyond or at least outside of those of us who do not ordinarily bear the responsibility of regular religious leadership. Even those of us who do bear such responsibility regularly, whether ordained or lay, often experience our public religious rituals as possessing authority beyond ourselves, deriving from a higher authority than we have, even if we are ordained. Within some liturgical Christian traditions, certain rites and ritual practices do have the force of law: these are called canonical practices, and the freedom individuals or groups have to alter them may be very limited indeed. In other Christian traditions, even where official liturgical rites may exist, they are not required, and there may be more freedom there for creation and innovation, even if it is not always taken.

It is true that established religious rituals are the creation of someone. Often they are the work of a group of individuals, joined together perhaps in time and space (a committee of church leaders, say, or a council of scholars), or maybe joined together across decades or centuries by common identity and common sources (as in the case of religious rituals whose origins are lost in time but which continue to be claimed and used in the ever-changing present). To put it another way, religious rituals do not just fall from the sky; they must be invented, at least once, by someone, whether an individual or group. Once we recognize this basic fact, we can begin to ask who invented this or that ritual, and for whom, and for what purpose. We can begin to explore how and why religious rituals come into being, we can ask whether an established religious ritual is true for us, and we can begin to see ourselves as creators of religious ritual.

All rituals are beyond our immediate control

Ritual that does what is needed, that gives shape and meaning to the experiences and events of our lives, that places us in touch with the divine, is ritual that "works." Anyone who has ever had the responsibility for planning or leading such a ritual knows the truth of the words of anthropologist William Harmon: "Ritual, once enacted, has a life of its own."[4]

We might call this awareness a "letting go," a process that recognizes the power of ritual to engage those participating in it at a deep level that goes beyond the simple control of any one of us. Metaphorically, we might think of the sailor at the tiller of a sailboat, adjusting sail and rudder in constant interplay with the wind and the water; the sailor who fails to recognize the power and direction of wind and wave is likely to capsize the boat. Or think of a skilled horseback rider, working in harmony with the power and energy and mind of the horse. The failure to recognize and work with the animal's power and will is similarly likely to result in a fall. A midwife attending a birth is definitely not the one "in control," but rather the one who observes, assesses, and assists the process, offering intervention when necessary. Similarly, the director of a play, who may be authoritative, even authoritarian, with the cast in rehearsal, must finally stand back during the performance and watch the actors perform without any direct interference.

All rituals are performances

Notice that all of these metaphors have this in common: they are types of performance. Those of us raised in and most familiar with the Western dominant culture's way of seeing the world have a tendency to think of religious worship as something that primarily (if not exclusively) engages our minds. But we may be somewhat embarrassed to admit that we have bodies, let alone that our bodies are primary places where religious activity takes place. Nevertheless, ritual of every kind, including Christian ritual, is irreducibly physical. Even the most passive worship service still assumes the physical presence of worshipers.

Furthermore, all rituals involve doing something, usually doing something with our bodies. Even if the "doing" is sitting, we remain embodied sitters, as it were. Moreover, in a ritual the sitting (or other "doing") is purposeful. It is performance in the simplest meaning of the word: to complete thoroughly or, in the words of Webster's dictionary, "to carry out, to do." To perform is to do something completely and thoroughly.

No two ritual events are identical

While it possible (and even commonplace) to repeat a ritual, it is impossible to duplicate it. This inescapable fact is, in truth, a blessing and a gift to the planners of a religious ritual event. It means that absolute control is not only undesirable, but also finally impossible. Within this always fresh space between the repetition and the new event works the power that is named the Holy Spirit in the Christian tradition. The Spirit blows where it will.

Ritual is a way of knowing

We tend to identify knowledge with ideas that we imagine as residing inside our heads, or at least inside our brains. But ritual reminds us of another form of knowing, what we can call ritual knowledge. Ritual knowledge is gained through physical bodily action. Think about how you learned to do anything that was primarily physical: learning a dance, perhaps, or learning to ride a bicycle. In the case of learning a dance, the music teaches your body how to do it; the bicycle teaches your body how to balance on it, how to move it forward, how to steer it and stop it. When you are dancing or riding a bicycle, you are attending to your body, or, better, your body is attending to itself through physical action. This corporeal, bodily learning is what we do when we ritualize. In ritual action, we are not primarily thinking and then moving (though we have seen plenty of ritual leaders whose wooden actions seem to suggest they cannot break free from overthinking what they are doing). We are engaging in "exploratory and experiential action," in the words of Theodore Jennings.[5] We are gaining ritual knowledge by engaging in ritual. And we engage in ritual primarily through our bodies.

A DISCIPLINE OF MAKING AND SETTING FREE

The purpose of this discipline is to practice the creative process of making and letting go.

All liturgies, even those taken from printed resources, require both invention and abandonment. Invention involves the adaptation and appropriation of something for a unique time and place. Abandonment involves setting the liturgy free to work its own power in the unique time and place, letting it go. While this is to some extent true of all work, it is particularly true of liturgy. This discipline can be undertaken by an individual or by a group such as a liturgy planning team or worship committee.

Step one: paying attention

We are regularly engaged in making things, from the ordinary and rather short-term activities of making a meal or raking a lawn to larger and more long-term work of creating liturgical events. The first step in developing a discipline of making and unmaking is paying attention to our own work, "practicing the presence of God," especially in our beginnings and letting go.

Step two: making

The creative work should be undertaken prayerfully, using one of the prayers above or some other appropriate prayer for beginning a creative project.

Step three: setting it free

When one's work on the effort is completed (the meal prepared, the lawn raked, the liturgy planned), it is necessary to bless the work and let it go. The meal is consumed, the leaves composted, the liturgy preparation completed. Say a prayer of letting go.

BASIC RITUAL PATTERNS

Rituals in their simplest form require only three elements: a focusing of attention, followed by a making or doing of something, and finally a letting go. Let us consider the several ways in which these three movements can be understood and employed in making ritual.

Focusing

The first step in any ritual, whether for use by an individual or by a group of any size, is a focusing of attention. The means of bringing about this focus are rich and varied, and the planners of a ritual should feel free to explore the full range of possibilities. Most familiar to those of us with long association with traditional worship is a verbal call to attention of some kind. In some traditions this might be called a "call to worship," or an opening prayer, or a declaration of purpose, or a litany or reading. Sometimes the community and its leader may engage in a verbal dialogue as a means of expressing this focusing of attention, but such verbal articulation is not required. What is required is that all present focus their attention on the common ritual work at hand. Nonverbal calls to attention are also possible: the medieval practice of ringing bells to call people to worship, the sounding of a gong or drum, the blowing of the shofar or trumpet. In short, any sound can serve to call people's attention to the common ritual work, or even simply to focus one's attention for private prayer or ritual.

Another means of focusing attention is through physical movement, gesture, or action of some kind. This might be as simple as entering the space designated for ritual, or as highly structured as making a religious gesture of some kind: bowing, making the sign of the cross or other meaningful gesture, lighting a candle, venerating an image, icon, or religious object. And of course, a ritual may begin with any combination of these elements.

Doing/making

The heart of any ritual is the doing or making of something. In a wedding ceremony, for example, we are making two separate people into a married couple. In Christian baptism, we are making someone into a Christian. In the Christian Eucharist, we are eating a holy meal together. A healing service intends to effect a healing of some kind, a blessing service brings about a blessing, and so on. The doing might be as simple as listening to the Holy One in silence or offering a brief thanksgiving or asking for help for ourselves or for others. The doing might be complex and multilayered, as in the case of Christian baptism, and involve several kinds of doing and making within a single event. Planners and leaders will want to consider carefully what it is that the liturgy is doing, and what it is making. Being clear about this, both with the planners and the worshipers, will give shape and purpose to a liturgical event.

Releasing

The final step in any ritual is a letting go, releasing the liturgical event into time and space. Tongan artist Filipe Tohi recites this chant as he creates his stone carvings:

> God of the heavens
> Creator of the land
> Creator of the mountains
> I stand here and wait
> You are the light
> Give me a glimpse of your presence
> So your countenance
> My carving will reflect
> Token of my appreciation

When he has completed his work, he offers this chant:

> The flower has bloomed
> The stone is carved
> For all to see
> Behold where it stands
> The stone waits
> Filled with the past
> For the children of tomorrow
> Stand up and proclaim
> To all the visitors
> The beginning of this
> And its accomplishment[6]

The truth that all liturgies and rituals are ultimately out of our immediate control means that the letting go, for the planners and leaders, begins at the beginning of the liturgical event. The necessity of trusting to one's planning—to the community enacting the liturgy and to the liturgy itself—requires both spiritual discipline and skill. The skill of releasing a liturgy as event can be learned through practice of a spiritual discipline of preparation and release, as described in the preceding section, "A Discipline of Making and Setting Free." But in addition to this broader practice of releasing control over a liturgical event, it is also necessary to ritualize the ending of a liturgy in order to signal the communal letting go and releasing of the community back into their daily lives.

This final liturgical step has often been ritualized as a blessing and dismissal, sometimes as a closing prayer or closing communal song. Or the community might be released through instrumental music, the traditional organ postlude, for example. In some parts of the ancient church, a major portion of the Sunday liturgy involved the dismissals, as groups of worshipers, at different times in the service, came forward and received an individual blessing in the form of laying on of hands by the presider of the liturgy. Indeed, from this elaborate series of dismissals the ancient liturgy acquired its name, "Mass," or, in Latin, *missa*, meaning dismissal. As with the calling to attention at the beginning of a liturgy, the releasing of the liturgical work and the community gathered to do that work can take a rich variety of forms, from the verbal blessing and dismissal to the nonverbal sound of a chime or bell, or a gesture such as mutual blessing.

PRAYERS FOR RITUAL PATTERNS
AND LITURGICAL PROCESS

A PRAYER OF BEGINNINGS

(This prayer can be used corporately or individually, at the beginning of a planning process or indeed the beginning of any creative work. The expanded version includes remembrance of God's creative work in the past. The short version simply invokes God who is both beginning and end of all things. Both offer the option of naming the specific work being undertaken.)

Brief version:

Holy One,
in you all things come into being,
and in you all things come to rest in the end.

Bless our beginnings
(especially this work),
bring our work to fulfillment,
and may it rest in you from beginning to end.

In the name of Jesus,
the alpha and omega, beginning and end,
and in the power of the Spirit who enlivens our work,
hear us, we pray.

Expanded version:

Holy One,
in you all things come into being,
and in you all things come to rest in the end.

In the beginning you called forth light, and earth, and every
    living thing.
The mountains rose at your voice, and the waters leaped and
    the trees danced.

In the beginning you made us to be like you
always making and making anew.

As each day begins earth's creation again,
as each breath begins our creation again,
so we begin this work.

Bless our beginnings
(especially this work),
bring our work to fulfillment,
and may it rest in you from beginning to end.

In the name of Jesus,
the alpha and omega, beginning and end,
and in the power of the Spirit who enlivens our work,
hear us, we pray.

❦

A PRAYER OF BEGINNINGS, ADDRESSED TO CHRIST

*(This brief prayer, addressed directly to Christ, who is Alpha and Omega,
can be used at the beginning of any effort as a reminder that everything
we begin, whether large project or small effort, is done in the ignorance
of its conclusion, but with confidence in Christ.)*

Alpha and Omega,
Womb and Grave,
fresh spring of water and endless sea,
you are the start of every journey
and its destination.

We begin now
but we cannot know the ending.
It is beyond our reach and our sight.

We know only
that all, all, all
begins and ends in you.

A Prayer of Letting Go

Out of our hands, Holy One,
we release this, the work of our hands.
Beyond our minds,
we release this work of our minds.
With the blessing of our hearts
we release this work of our hearts.

RESOURCES FOR RITUAL PATTERNS

Black, Kathy. *Culturally Conscious Worship*. St. Louis, Mo.: Chalice Press, 2000.

_____. *Worship Across Cultures: A Handbook*. Nashville: Abingdon Press, 1998.

Carnes, Robin Deen, and Sally Craig. *Sacred Circles: A Guide to Creating Your Own Women's Spirituality Group*. San Francisco: HarperSanFrancisco, 1998.

Driver, Tom F. *Liberating Rites: Understanding the Transformative Power of Ritual*. Boulder, Colo.: Westview Press, 1998.

Gottlieb, Lynn. *She Who Dwells Within: A Feminist Vision of a Renewed Judaism*. San Francisco: HarperSanFrancisco, 1995.

Grimes, Ronald L. "Emerging Ritual," in *Reading, Writing, and Ritualizing*. Washington, D.C.: Pastoral Press, 1993.

_____. "Liturgical Supinity, Liturgical Erectitude," in *Reading, Writing, and Ritualizing*.

Jennings, Theodore W., Jr. "On Ritual Knowledge," in *Readings in Ritual Studies*. Ed. Ronald L. Grimes. Upper Saddle River, N.J.: Prentice-Hall, 1995.

Procter-Smith, Marjorie. "Feminist Ritual Strategies: The Ekklesia Gynaikon at Work," in *Toward a New Heaven and a New Earth: Essays in Honor of Elisabeth Schüssler Fiorenza*. Ed. Fernando Segovia. Maryknoll, N.Y.: Orbis Press, 2003.

THREE

Places

Wisdom has built her house,
she has hewn her seven pillars.

— Proverbs 9:1

THINKING ABOUT SACRED PLACES

The guiding image of this book, expressed in its title, is a spatial one: the church in her house. It bespeaks creation of sacred place ("church") within ordinary space ("house"). It connects the public vocation of the church as *ekklesia*, the gathering of free people to make decisions for the well-being of the whole world, with the struggle of women and other oppressed peoples for freedom and dignity: in HER house. Virginia Woolf wrote famously of women's need for "a room of one's own," and feminist Christian communities experience the need for a church place of our own, a church in her house. The need for physical space, a place we can claim and make our own and in which we can feel free is fundamental to our spiritual well-being. The biblical model for this place is found in the image of Wisdom's house.

Space and Place

Geographer Yi-Fu Tuan draws a useful distinction between space and place:

> Space is more abstract than place. What begins as undifferentiated space becomes place as we get to know it better and endow it with value. . . . If we think of space as that which allows movement then place is pause; each pause in movement makes it possible for location to be transformed into place.[7]

Our need for "a room (or church) of our own" is a need for both space and place, as Tuan delineates them. We whose movements have been curtailed and limited need space in which to move. We who have been denied the power to endow our own spaces with value need places to pause in safety and freedom.

Wisdom's house is open to all, built on the strong support of seven pillars, a place of freedom and beauty. Its open space welcomes those who seek understanding and want to learn the ways of wisdom. How can we find this place, and how will we know it when we find it? Or perhaps we will not find it ready made but must build it ourselves, in partnership with one another and with Wisdom herself. Or perhaps the process includes some combination of seeking, finding, and building.

Another way of thinking about sacred places draws on Christian thinking about creation, and especially the earth as God's good creation. The creation story in Genesis can be understood as an example of Tuan's distinction between space and place. In the beginning, all was space, abstract and undifferentiated, "a formless void." And as God pauses over each element of the world, this empty space is transformed into place: light and dark, waters and dry land, plants and animals and human beings, all in their sacred place, this good earth. Our tendency to separate sacred space from profane space, to name some places holy and others ordinary, must be called into question by this creation story. And as we think about the places we gather to worship God, we remember that all the earth and all of creation beyond our earth has already been made sacred because God has paused there and has endowed these places with value and meaning. As we claim certain places as sacred to us, it is important that we remember the original holiness of all places and of the sacred connections that join us with all creation.

Some sacred places do come to us ready made, either by significant and powerfully meaningful events or by long usage as a sacred place. The Church of the Holy Sepulchre in Jerusalem, for centuries understood to be the place of Jesus' crucifixion and burial, draws its power from the significance of these events for millions of Christians. The Wyoming fence where twenty-one-year-old gay man Matthew Shepard was beaten and left for dead in 1998 becomes a sacred place, marked with stones in the form of a cross and hallowed by memorial gifts. Churches and chapels, from the magnificence of Notre Dame cathedral in Paris to the spare modesty of Blooming Grove Methodist Church in rural central Texas, reverberate with holiness for those who pay attention. Other sacred places reveal themselves to us, sometimes as a result of our own earnest seeking, sometimes as gift and surprise.

A SPIRITUAL DISCIPLINE OF SACRED PLACES:
Feminist Ritual Pathways to Sacred Space

This practice may be undertaken individually or in a group. Making notes or journaling will aid you in developing a spiritual practice of place.

The feminist ritual pathways outlined in chapter 1 can help guide us to the sacred places where Wisdom meets us, to the church in her house. These pathways may be understood metaphorically, as a basis for discussion or personal reflection. But it is always best to put one-self physically on a path in and through sacred places in order to come to a wiser understanding of the meaning and power of such places.

First, there is the pathway of women's experience. This is a path-way that leads through places to which we have been denied access: the altar, the pulpit, the classroom, the academic seminar, the places of religious power and authority. At these places we recognize and lament the history and ongoing story of denial of access for women to these places. Have you been in such places? Have you attempted to enter them? Is your experience one of access or denial? Do you know of some who were denied sacred places to which you had access?

As we follow this path, we decide whether to claim these places for ourselves and others who have been denied, or whether we must keep moving on beyond these historic places of power. Sometimes the simple act of putting our bodies into the physical places historically denied to us can be a powerful ritual: taking our place behind the altar or stepping into the pulpit. This path also takes us to the secret, hid-den places where women have encountered the Holy One under the constraints of kyriarchal ordering. Where access to places of power is limited or denied, women and others have found the Holy One in hid-den places, in the private sphere of the domestic space, in the hush ar-bors of the slave, in kitchen and nursery and barn and field and street and alley and factory. Do you know the stories of some of these hid-den sacred places? Have you been sheltered by them at times?

At times these despised and rejected people have defied their limitations, formed their own communities, claimed their own sa-cred places, challenged the kyriarchal barriers, and resisted their own marginalization. The church in her house is sometimes hidden and secret, sometimes openly defiant. Regardless, always these places of encounter with the Holy One bespeak our restlessness with things as they are and articulate our hope for a time when such barriers and limitations no longer exist. In the words of Anne Cameron, we are always "dreaming of a place not like this one."[8]

The second feminist Christian pathway goes through the sacred places that are our bodies. Our bodies become the locus of encounter with the Holy One when we attend to the places our bodies have been, when we choose where we place our bodies, when we let our bodies show us sacred places in the world. These places may be commemorative, recalling and reminding us of the cycles of meaning embedded in our women's bodies, cycles of menses, pregnancy, birth, menopause, and cycles of growth, fertility, life, and death. But our bodies also bear the memory of fear, threat, and harm. Such memories demand that we find a prophetic place for our bodies, and that our bodies themselves be prophetic places. What are your body's memories?

We may commemorate our bodies' wisdom in rituals celebrating our bodily cycles, or we may put our bodies in places that proclaim our refusal to continue to allow women and other vulnerable ones to suffer. The path of our bodies may lead to intimate, even private, rituals, or it may lead us to public places of protest against war, against sexual and domestic violence, against hate crimes, against discrimination toward gay, lesbian, and bisexual people, toward persons with disabilities, toward the poor, children, the aged. By putting our sacred but despised bodies in place, and by paying attention with our bodies, we can be led into sacred places where Wisdom dwells and we can embody the ekklesia of women.

The path of women's bodies leads us also into the path of suffering and struggle. Places of healing, of protest, of lament and loss lie along this path and call out to us. Wherever despised and rejected bodies suffer, struggle, and rise up in the power of the Spirit, there Wisdom's house is found. Where have these places of sacred struggle been for you? Where communities of resistance have gathered, where people of good will work for the well-being of all living creatures, there the ekklesia of women is engaged in its holy work. Where have you encountered this holy work?

And intersecting with all the other paths, the Christian feminist pathway of relationships with other women, with all who suffer and struggle with us for freedom and joy, leads us to seek common ground. Although the expression "common ground" is most often used metaphorically, in this context we mean it quite literally. Wisdom's house is wide open to all, a seven-pillared open space to encounter the Holy One. The church in her house must be literally "common ground," a place for the gathering of all who seek Wisdom's gifts. When we seek sacred places for our prayer and ritual, it is essential that the space be open and welcoming, lacking barriers, closed doors, or steep stairs. Where have you had a glimpse of such holy "common ground"? As you imagine Wisdom's house, what are the "seven pillars" that you see that uphold the life and work of Wisdom's house?

And then there are the pathways that lead into untracked space, limitless mystery that calls out to be the focus of our spiritual attention or that at first appears to be devoid of holiness and power. If we imagine that we already know where all feminist pathways can take us, we risk missing the mystery of revelation, the discovery of previously unknown territory and unrecognized sacred places. When have you been surprised by the spiritual wisdom and power of a place you had not recognized as sacred before it revealed itself to you? When have you sought the mystery and discovery of the untracked pathway, and where did this pathway lead?

As we follow these feminist Christian pathways to seek the sacred places to house our prayers and liturgies, we find signposts, markers left behind for us by those who have traveled these paths before. These signposts can help us to know when we have found Wisdom's house. Here are some basics that can help us when choosing or finding or creating sacred places for worship.

1. *Sacred places can be created.* Pay attention to places in the world, and especially in your local environment, where the Holy One seems to be manifest. The Holy One may be found in places of great suffering or in places of great joy. In such places, the prayers and liturgies are called forth by the place itself and its significance.

2. *Sacred places can make themselves known to you.* By paying careful attention to a particular space, whether enclosed or in the open air, it is possible to learn to discern the best place for a ritual to take place. It will be important to take into account the size of the gathering and the purpose of the event. In these circumstances, the place can be determined by the ritual need. A baptism, for example, requires the presence of water but does not necessarily require a baptismal font. Any container will do, whether a natural water site, such as a river, stream, or lake, or a human-made container, from a swimming pool to a handheld bowl.

3. *Finding sacred places requires paying attention.* It may be useful to designate certain members of the community to be responsible for locating sacred places and to encourage them to develop rituals and prayers for this work, such as those provided in the following section. We might call this responsibility geomancy, a term meaning discerning the power inherent in places on the earth, and the person serving in this capacity the geomancer. Even communities that have their own designated space for worship will benefit from giving attention to the best way to make use of the space for a given liturgy. An individual who has set aside a special place for personal prayer can enrich her prayer by focusing on the place itself. If ritual in itself is "a mode of paying attention," as Jonathan Z. Smith[9] argues, the place where a ritual "takes place" becomes a "focusing lens" for giving attention to the Holy One. The geomancer is one who learns to focus the lens with sensitivity and accuracy.

4. *Sacred places are ordinary places that make room for the extraordinary.* There is nothing found in religious space that is not already part of the everyday world in which we live: table, chairs, washbasin, light, bread, wine, water, and pictures or images. It is their use in liturgy that gives the ordinary a sacramental meaning, and it is their familiarity that shows us the holiness of daily life. Becoming attuned to this interplay between the ordinary and the extraordinary can assist in the discovery and creation of sacred places for worship.

◈   PATTERNS FOR SACRED PLACES   ◈

No, it doesn't have to be a circle. Feminist Christian prayer and liturgy can happen in any configuration you can think of. But attention to the arrangement of the space can enhance and enable the work of the Spirit in the liturgy, no less in the prayer of an individual than in a gathering of tens, hundreds, or thousands.

Worship is a sensory experience; it is a physical, bodily experience. This is the primary reason one gives attention to the space in which we pray and worship. We worship and pray with our whole selves, with our bodies and our bodies' senses, as well as with our minds. And because our bodies reside in place and our senses receive information from the environment, the physical space in which we pray and worship helps to shape our prayer and ritual, as it helps to orient and direct our thoughts.

In some ways, this is literally true. It is at least very difficult, and perhaps impossible, to do a circle dance in a room filled with immoveable furniture. It invites body-mind dissociation to speak of our prayers rising like incense (Ps. 141) without the scent and sight of rising fragrant smoke.

But the space in which we pray and worship works on us more subtly as well. Let's begin with mundane questions of design and arrangement of space. Will there be seating in pews or in chairs or on the floor? In rows, in a circle, facing forward, or inward? Natural or artificial light? In established worship space, alternative public space, or private space? Indoors or outdoors? Will seating be provided or will participants stand for the liturgy? Some guidelines can help planners make these decisions.

Work with the space you have

One writer, speaking out of many years of experience with feminist prayer groups, observed that "as soon as they enter a space in which they are going to meet, some members of the group will start rearranging the furniture." A conventional Christian worship space may lack flexibility, preventing or seriously limiting some kinds of ritual activities. But if that is the space you have and major changes are not possible, you will need to make the space work for you. Remember that Wisdom calls at the crossroads and at the gates (Prov. 8:1–3); we can make use of the space available, and claim space set aside for others as our own. In claiming this place for our own, however, we are free to rearrange the furniture to meet our needs.

Step off the path

In order to claim an existing space, we may need to reorient ourselves, moving outside of the normal established pathways. Don't adapt your worship to existing space; adjust the space to accommodate you. The space exists for the people, not the people for the space. If the space won't accommodate the people, either in numbers or in the ritual needs of the community, perhaps you will need to seek another sacred place. Is there a center aisle? To what alternative use can this open space be put? Can it be a space for dance or movement, or can altars or other ritual centers be placed there? Is there a narthex or entryway that might serve as an alternative worship center? These spaces are often open and more flexible than pew-filled chancels or seat-filled auditoriums, and they may serve well if your group will fit in the space. Identify any "invisible" places, areas of the worship space that are not used or are underused for some reason. Can they be claimed as worship space? If you are planning to use a public space, such as a meeting room, special care will need to be taken to claim the institutional space for holy use. In a private home, the domestic atmosphere can serve as the basis for the use of the space, but accommodations for gathering and movement will need to be made. Domestic spaces are designed primarily for sitting, resting, eating. Worship of the Holy One may often demand more space for movement, gathering, and physical activity.

Seating is optional

Many of us are so accustomed to associating sitting in pews with Christian worship that we forget that churches did not have permanent pews in the West until the eighteenth century, and most Eastern rite churches still do not. While it will be important to accommodate those who will need seating for health or other reasons, there are many ritual advantages to leaving the worship space free of chairs or pews, if possible. It frees participants up to move about, it encourages planners to consider incorporating congregational movement in the liturgy, it permits establishing multiple worship centers, or foci, it enables nonsequential ritual, and it allows individuals to choose the level and locus of participation. Feminist emancipatory liturgy is active, democratically participatory, and embodied. The open space of Wisdom's house is fully accessible and welcoming.

Make room to move

Whatever the configuration of the space that is given, find ways to enable movement by the participants. Moving from place to place within an enclosed space, or outdoors in private or public space, embodies the radical democracy of feminist emancipatory prayer and liturgy. It enhances the possibility of engaging our bodies, in all their wondrous diversity and uniqueness, as vehicles for and manifestations of the holy. Remember that the movement of our bodies from place to place may include the space needed for wheelchairs, walkers, guide animals, and other adjustments. In the common ground of Wisdom's house, full access by all is essential. Specific details and measurements for the space needed to accommodate wheelchairs can be found, for example, in *Accessibility Audit for Churches* (Board of Global Ministries, United Methodist Church, 1995).

Make the place beautiful

Dressing the space can be very elaborate and time-consuming or simple and inexpensive. The objective of dressing the space, however, is not to draw attention to the decorative elements themselves, but to beautify and make hospitable the place in which the ekklesia gathers and to foster a strong sense of prayer and community. The same spiritual discipline that teaches us to identify and shape holy places can also help us discern how to arrange the furnishings of worship space in ways that focus attention on its holiness. The use of objects of meaning and beauty can be an important aspect of this, but first attention must be given to the accessibility of the space, which is made beautiful first of all by those who gather in it to worship in the Spirit. Then the space must be arranged in ways suitable to the event. This might mean the use of plenty of natural or artificial light. Or it might mean a space that can be darkened, to be lighted with candles or lamps. Or it might mean making a table or a container of water central to the space.

PRAYERS FOR HOLY PLACES

A Prayer for a Geomancer

Holy Wisdom, open my heart.
Holy Wisdom, guide my feet.
Holy Wisdom, show me your house of joy and hope.

A Blessing of a Place of Private Prayer

(Walking about the boundaries of the space)
Holy Wisdom, build your house in this place.
Establish your pillars in my presence,
open the doors of my heart;
blow through the open windows of my mind
in this place
in this place.

(Touching, sitting, or lying on the floor of the space)
Holy Wisdom, establish your house on this ground.
Plant me in your rich soil;
plow the field of my heart
in this place
in this place.

(Placing hands on one's breast and pausing to take deep breaths)
Holy Wisdom, fill your house with this air, your breath.
Enter me with each deep breath;
swim in my bloodstream,
beat in my heart
in this place
in this place.

A PRAYER IN A SACRED PLACE OF NATURAL BEAUTY

In this beautiful place
I see you, Holy One.
Your blessings fill my heart
in this beautiful place.

☾

A PRAYER IN A SACRED PLACE OF GREAT SUFFERING AND STRUGGLE

Holy One,
witness our tears, our cries of sorrow
at the great suffering in this place.
Bring an end to this suffering,
bless this struggle,
hear our cry
in this holy place.

☾

A SERVICE OF BLESSING OF A GATHERING PLACE
Orienting a Holy Place in the Universe

(Let the community gather outside the place to be set aside for use for worship. Begin with all facing in the direction of the sun. A single leader may read the declaration for each direction, or one for each direction.)

Bless the Holy One, clothed with beauty, wrapped in light as
    with a garment (Ps. 104:1–2).
Her steadfast love endures forever.

(Let the community turn 90 degrees to the right.)

The Holy One covers the heavens with clouds, prepares rain
    for the earth, makes grass grow on the hills (Ps. 47:8).
Her steadfast love endures forever.

(Let the community turn facing away from the sun.)

Your justice is like the mighty mountains, your judgments
    are like the great deep; you save humans and animals
    alike (Ps. 36:6).
Her steadfast love endures forever.

(Let the community turn another 90 degrees to the right.)

With you is the fountain of life; in your light we see light
    (Ps. 36:9).
Her steadfast love endures forever.

*(Let the community face inward toward one another and gaze upward at
the sky.)*

Your steadfast love, Holy One, is higher than the heavens.
And your faithfulness reaches to the clouds (Ps. 108:4).
Her steadfast love endures forever.

(Let the community gaze at or touch the ground beneath our feet.)

When you send forth your Spirit, Holy One, we are created,
and you renew the face of the ground (Ps. 104:30).
Her steadfast love endures forever.

(Let the community gaze at one another's faces.)

Wisdom rejoices in the inhabited world, delighting in the
    human race (Prov. 8:31).
Her steadfast love endures forever.

Entering Wisdom's House

(Let the community gather just inside the doorway to the worship space.)

Doorways are sacred to women for we
are the doorways of life and we must choose
what comes in and what goes out.[10]

(Let the community walk or dance around the boundaries of the space to be set apart, singing, chanting, or playing instruments; this may be done single file, or in a circle dance, as the space permits. The following or some other suitable text may be sung or chanted:)

Holy Wisdom, build your house in this place.

(Let the community gather in the center of the worship space, facing one another.)

Wisdom has built her house,
she has hewn her seven pillars.

(Let seven speakers name each of the seven pillars that will support the work of this community and gathering, prepared as part of the spiritual discipline of the community. After each speaker concludes, all respond by saying/singing:)

Holy Wisdom, build your house in this place.

(Let the table host move to the community table, inviting the rest of the community to gather around. Members of the community may bring the bread and wine and other things needed to set the table at this time. The table host may read Wisdom's Invitation and the Great Thanksgiving, or the reading may be shared among those present.)

Wisdom has slaughtered her animals,
she has mixed her wine,
she has also set her table.
She has sent out her women ministers.
She calls from the high places,
come, eat of my bread,
drink of the wine I have mixed.
Lay aside immaturity, and live,
and walk in the way of insight.

May God be with you.
And with you too.
Lift up your hearts.
We lift them to the holy one.

Let us give thanks to God in this place.
It is good to give thanks.

Holy One of Wisdom,
we give you thanks for bringing us together in this place.
You established the foundations of the earth,
and set the boundaries of the sea.
Your wisdom upholds the world,
your path leads to understanding.
All earth's creatures are in your care,
and you delight in your human children.

Even when we have turned away from your pathways
you have come after us, searching the streets
and calling us to your banquet table.

And so, with all your creation
and your prophets of every age, we sing:

Holy, Holy, Holy
God of blessing and giver of wisdom,
earth, sea, and sky are full of your beauty.
Blessed are all who come in your name.
Blessings in the highest.

Holy are you, and blessed is your prophet Jesus,
child of Mary, friend of humankind.
He traveled by your paths and taught your wisdom to all.
Poor himself, to the poor he offered hope;
oppressed unto death, to the oppressed he announced freedom.

The night when he was betrayed to death,
Jesus, your prophet, once again called the wise to your table,
and took bread in his hands.

Lifting up his eyes to heaven he gave you thanks
and broke the bread and gave it to them, saying,
"Take and eat. This bread is my body.
Whenever you do this remember me."
Come, eat of my bread.
And after the meal he took the cup, gave you thanks, and said,
"Drink from this. This is the new covenant in my blood.
Whenever you do this, remember me."
Come, drink of the wine I have mixed.

Remembering Jesus, therefore,
we offer these gifts of bread and wine and ourselves
in this holy place.

Send the power of your strong Spirit
on these gifts and on us gathered in this holy place.
Make this meal, this place, and this people
holy and blessed, true signs of your presence in the world.
Come, Holy Wisdom, build your house in this place.
Through your prophet Jesus Christ,
in your holy and strong Spirit
in this holy place,
now and always.
Amen.

(Let the meal be shared among all those present, in joy and peace. At the conclusion of the meal, the community may once again move about the place, singing and dancing. If any food or drink remains from the meal, it may be taken outside and returned to the earth from which it came to nourish the creatures of earth.)

Holy Wisdom, build your house in this place.

RESOURCES FOR SPACE AND PLACES

King, Eileen. "A Lingering Question: What Is Feminist Prayer?" In *Women at Worship: Interpretations of North American Diversity.* Ed. Marjorie Procter-Smith and Janet R. Walton. Louisville: Westminster John Knox Press, 1993.

Maitland, Sara. *A Map of the New Country: Women and Christianity.* Boston: Routledge, 1983.

Smith, Jonathan Z. *To Take Place: Toward Theory in Ritual.* Chicago: University of Chicago Press, 1987.

Tuan, Ti-Fu. *Topophilia: A Study of Environmental Perception, Attitudes, and Values.* Englewood Cliffs, N.J.: Prentice-Hall, 1974.

Vosko, Richard S. *God's House Is Our House: Re-imagining the Environment for Worship.* Collegeville, Minn.: Liturgical Press, 2006.

FOUR

THINGS

[A]s he sat at the table,
a woman came with an alabaster jar of very costly ointment of nard,
and she broke open the jar
and poured the ointment on his head.

—Mark 14:3

THINKING ABOUT HOLY THINGS

"Holy things for holy people." Does the Christian belief in the incarnation include the entire physical world? Are physical things capable of conveying the presence and power of God, or are they merely inert matter? Worship inevitably involves matter; it is always physical and always includes people, the space people occupy, and material objects. Perception of the holy can be either fostered or hindered by the presence of matter, the "stuff" of worship. Indeed, this very physicality of worship, its embodiment in ourselves and the material world in which we live and move and interact, can be a window into transcendence. It can literally put us in the way of the Holy; it can show us the pathway and in fact become that pathway to the Holy.

When thinking about holy things, we remember above all that we human beings are creatures of earth. We are not above, or beyond, or greater than the matter that is the world, but we are a part of it. We are creatures of earth, which means that earth owns us, we do not own earth. To be owned by the earth is to be mortal, to cling to all that is mortal but to let go in time. This great truth, that we are the earth's creatures, is reflected, among other places, in the ancient Christian burial rite: "ashes to ashes, dust to dust," the handful of dirt thrown into the grave, the armful of flowers, the recognition that in death we rest in dirt, earth reclaims us. As it does every day, with every breath, with every movement, not only for us and our fragile and beautiful bodies, but with all that lives as part of earth, both animate and inanimate.

So before we consider what objects and materials we will include in our liturgies or how we will use them, we do well first to contemplate our kinship with the whole material world. We do well to remember that we, like the things we use in our liturgy, are creatures of earth. We are not masters or rulers or in some way independent of earth. We humans are small beings who share our existence as creatures of earth with many others, some like us, some unlike.

An awareness of this kinship with all that is, even with inanimate things, can guide and inform the way we choose and handle them in liturgy. Consider: without the font, whether a simple bowl or large pool or natural river or lake, we have no container for water; and without water, which must be contained in some way, we have no means of baptism. Our very identity as baptized Christians depends on things both natural and made by human hands. Or consider: without the cup, the plate, the table, we have no container for wine and bread; without the human effort that produces cup and plate and table, and wine and bread, we have no holy meal that nurtures and sustains us in the Christian life. Our ongoing life in community depends on things both natural (grapes and grain) and made by human hands. Or consider: without the soil and sun and rain, we have no grapes and grain for the holy meal; without the clay or wood or metal or stone, we have no cup or plate or table.

The existence of water, of soil and sun and rain and trees, depends not on us, but on the mystery of creation itself. It is this mystery that gives rise to the Christian notion of sacraments. The Latin word *sacramentum*, originally meaning a vow or promise, was used to translate the Greek word *mysterion*, which we recognize as the root of the English word mystery. The Christian sacraments of bread and wine, of baptismal water, reveal the promise of the Holy One and of the essential goodness of creation. In these earthly things, we perceive with our senses the very mystery of the Holy One. We experience the wonder of creation, the good creation of which we are but a small part.

In considering our relation to all that is, as small members and not as rulers, we remember, literally, our humble connection with the earth. The root of the word humility is humus—earth, soil. And it is this good earth that grounds and nurtures us and, at the last, receives us. Each time we choose and handle a physical object, we open ourselves to the holiness that resides within all that is; we encounter the Creator of all that is.

All rituals assume the use of things, of physical objects. In the case of traditional Christian liturgy, the central objects (bread, wine or grape juice, water, oil) receive the most attention and are understood to be sacraments, sacred things, themselves. In addition to these, other objects, such as the containers for the sacramental objects (fonts and bowls for water, cups and plates for bread and wine, dishes and bottles for oil), and supplementary objects such as candles, images, textiles, flowers, and furniture are also part of traditional liturgies. Feminist liturgies frequently expand the list of sacred objects used to include natural objects such as shells and stones, bird feathers, leaves, and seeds as well as created objects, especially objects made by or representing the lives and stories of women. Often these created objects reflect women's traditional culture in the form of linens, embroidery, quilts, and other needlework art. The traditional Christian meal of bread and wine is sometimes expanded in feminist liturgies to include other foods as well as, or in place of, these traditional objects, but the traditional sacramental foods of bread and wine themselves already link us to women's traditional culture with food preparation at its heart.

A SPIRITUAL DISCIPLINE OF HOLY THINGS:
A Practice of Paying Attention

Learning to pay attention to things, seeking to see their holiness, requires, above all, time. The first step, then, in paying attention is to slow down. Slow the breathing, quiet the mind, still the body. The second step is to reduce distractions. Still extraneous noise and eliminate unnecessary visual clutter. The third step is to focus. Slowing the breathing, quieting the mind, stilling the body, reducing audible and visual distraction—together these set the stage for focusing on the holy thing being contemplated. When these steps are taken, one may give over one's focus to the holy thing.

There are many simple ways of putting this discipline into practice. A walk through a park or even on a busy sidewalk can become an opportunity to practice paying attention. Slow your steps and take your time. Put aside busy thoughts that take you elsewhere, and focus on your immediate surroundings. Sharpen your eyes, attune your ears to your surroundings, and let them show you the beauty and holiness of things.

Another valuable practice that can help develop the ability to pay attention is gardening. This practice requires the discipline of hard physical work in combination with attentiveness to soil, water, air, wildlife (including birds and insects), and, of course, the plants themselves.

Bird watching or other wildlife observation adds to these basic disciplines the requirement of patience. Being willing to wait attentively for wildlife to appear is an important avenue for developing the spiritual discipline of paying attention to holy things. It also serves as a salutary reminder that we in ourselves or even in our humanity are not in charge of things.

Learning to give prayerful attention to holy things may require the disciplined use of the eyes, the ears, the hands, and even the whole body. The following exercises offer a few ways of practicing this discipline. You will discover your own ways of disciplining yourself to attend to the holy things of the world.

1. Plant a seed in a pot of soil or small plot of earth. Set aside a specific time each day (at least five full minutes: set a timer) to give your full attention to the (invisible) seed as it sprouts and grows. During this time, set aside distractions as much as possible and give your full attention to the growing seed.

2. Set aside a daily time to sit outdoors and contemplate the world in your immediate view. This may be on your porch or at a window. The view is less important than your attentive observation and contemplation.

3. Take a walk in your immediate neighborhood. Look for small objects (stones, feathers, shards of glass, etc.) that speak to you. If it is appropriate, take the object or objects with you for ongoing contemplation. Let the object(s) speak to you.

4. Take a piece of fruit (apple, pear, etc.) and wash it slowly, paying attention to its shape and feel, its texture and distinctive marks. With a small knife, peel and slice the fruit and eat it slowly, experiencing its uniqueness and its beauty.

PATTERNS OF SACRAMENTS AND MYSTERIES

The word sacrament, in Latin *sacramentum*, literally means "vow." It was used to translate a more powerful and suggestive Greek word, *mysterion*, or mystery.

The Mystery of Water, Wine, and Bread

The traditional Christian sacraments of baptism and eucharist employ common substances—water, wine, and bread—that in their sacramental usages reveal to us special meanings and messages about God.

Look for the commonplace

In considering the traditional sacramental things of baptism and eucharist, we remind ourselves of the essential ordinariness of these things. Centuries of Christian tradition have overlaid these simple things with an aura of uniqueness, seen them as set apart from the ordinary, and treated them differently from things we use in our daily lives. But consider the opposite movement: what if these things— water, bread, and wine—were chosen first because of their ordinariness? What could be more common than water? What more basic than bread? What more common to most of the world's people than wine? If the water of baptism is holy water, does that make it different from ordinary water, or does its holiness reveal the essential holiness of all water? True, different cultures use and make these common things—water, food, drink—in ways that are distinct to their environment; these differences are a source of sacramental understanding as well, a source of insight into the mystery of holy things.

Look for the beautiful

Beauty is subjective and culturally bound, and we begin to perceive the holiness of things when we open ourselves to beauty that takes unexpected forms. Here is another way the mystery of holy things can reveal itself to us. The use of beautiful things should take into account the circumstances of their creation. Are they the product of exploitation of human labor or of animals? Does their creation produce environmental pollution or disruption? Pay attention to the source of the sacramental things. Are local water sources unpolluted and available to all? Do bread and wine come from nonpolluting makers? Are they organic in origin or do they contribute to pollution of our common earth?

Value simplicity and function

Much traditional church decoration has tended toward the ornate and elaborate. When choosing objects to be used in worship, ask yourself, "What is this for?" and "How will it be used?" If it is functional and simple, it will be beautiful in its use. Attending to simplicity and function ensures that the things will be transparent to mystery rather than objects to be admired in themselves. Let the water be water, without elaborate containers or obscuring screens. Let the bread be bread, food that is eaten. Let the wine (fermented or unfermented) be what it is, drink that refreshes and renews. Let the function of the water of baptism as a cleansing bath be clear. Let the function of the bread and wine as food be clearly expressed in their form as well as their use.

Consider context

Any object to be used in worship should be appropriate for the particular context in which it will be used. That is, the social and cultural context as well as the character of the worshiping community must be taken into account. The things should seem natural and familiar as well as revelatory and in some sense mysterious. They might invite us into another reality or context than our own, but they should not be so alien as to be distracting.

Found Mysteries: Oil, Salt, and Other Things

Beyond the simple basic Christian sacraments lie many other holy things. Like the traditional sacraments, these objects too may reveal to us the mystery of the Holy One and the Wisdom of God. Some of these things have historical origins in Christian worship; others can be found by those who are attentive to the holiness of things.

Discover the power of ancient symbols and signs

Oil as a symbol and effective sign predates Christian worship by many centuries. Oil's healing power led to its use both medicinally and ritually and now perfumed oils are readily available. Contemporary use of scented oils suggests less of medicinal use and more of self-care use, and thus oils are a valuable part of a blessing service. Scented oils can be used in healing services to great effect, recalling the unnamed woman who anointed Jesus' head with fragrant ointment. But oil also connects us with our Christian vocation: to be Christian is to be anointed, and therefore the ancient use of oil in baptism can also be expanded to use in any liturgy that includes recognition or appointment in any Christian vocation, ordained or otherwise. Likewise, salt is an ancient symbol that is in much less contemporary use than oil. In the ancient world, before refrigeration, salt was a preservative and purifier as well as seasoning. Hence the use of salt in ancient rites of exorcism. Salt's purifying and preserving character makes it a powerful symbol in liturgies of purification, exorcism, and empowerment. It can be scattered on the ground, added to water, or placed on the tongue.

Make thoughtful use of candles

Candles have become so ubiquitous in worship that their power is very nearly lost. Light is a very powerful symbol, primordial in its effect, and can connect us with what is probably our earliest memory: moving from darkness of the womb to the light. But candles are neither the only possible use of light in liturgy nor always a necessity. The act of lighting candles can be a powerful symbolic act if tied logically to the ritual in which they are used. The use of a single large candle in the midst of a darkened space can convey hope, courage, and peace. The use of a candle before an image or object can become a focus for meditation. The use of many small candles, either hand-held or placed about a space, can focus attention or convey the power of individuals in community or can serve as visible prayers. But as with all things used in worship, it is important to ask, "What is this for?" and "How will it be used?" when choosing to use candles in a liturgy.

Be open to discovering new holy things in nature

One with disciplined attention can discover holy things in our midst: a stone, a shell, a feather, a blade of grass or a flower seed:

these and many other gifts of the earth can become powerful religious symbols, rightly understood. As signs of our connection with the earth, our partnership with all created things, the Creator's bounty and mystery, and our literal humility, natural things can be an important part of worship. As in the case of any holy thing used in worship, simplicity and usefulness are important considerations.

Seek holy things made by human hands

The use of human artifacts in worship is inevitable and necessary. Appropriate respect for the human creator of the object, and for that person's well-being, is essential to the use of such things, lest we participate, knowingly or unknowingly, in the oppression of others. Examples of such human artifacts range from practical items such as vessels for bread and wine and water, for oil and salt and candles and any other substance, table and chairs and other necessary furnishings, and linens of various kinds, to symbolic items such as crosses, banners, images, and the like. The needs of the liturgy at hand and the context of the worshiping community will determine the appropriateness of human artifacts for worship. It is always fitting for the needful things to be made by members of the worshiping community. This honors the creativity of the community and locates the liturgical recognition of these gifts firmly in the local context.

Seek the use of holy things that support justice and peace and the well-being of the human and natural environment

Care can be taken to use human artifacts that do not degrade the environment or human lives and that in fact support and encourage their well-being. Fair trade goods, environmentally responsible materials, and nonexploitive working conditions of the creators should be investigated and taken seriously when choosing things and materials to be used in worship. Such responsibility is in accord with the house of Holy Wisdom, open to and inviting to all.

Be creative and imaginative

Do not be constrained by what has been used in the past, either in your tradition or in your local community. The world is large and diverse, and Christian use of sacramental things in liturgy is wide and varied. The history of the Christian use of things in worship shows a lively appropriation of the familiar and the commonplace, an awareness of the mystery that resides in all that is. Be open.

Some Useful Holy Things to Find and Keep

Handsome tablecloths, napkins, and table runners can beautify a simple table for a holy meal. Large bolts of yard goods can also be useful and can serve multiple purposes; they might be draped over tables, hung from windows or rafters, or even wrapped around individuals being recognized or honored in some way. In ancient times, church linens were simple and modeled after clothes of common people. The best and newest clothes were saved for special occasions (Easter and Christmas and other holy days) and the older and worn linens were used during ordinary or penitential times. This principle works better than rigidly following an arbitrary seasonal color scheme. Cloth is a simple and inexpensive way to transform a space that might also be used for other purposes into a sacred space. It can also express a community's identity, ethical commitments, and connections with others around the world.

As with linens, simple dishes for ordinary occasions and special ones for special occasions are more authentic than expensive vessels made of precious metals. For holy meals, a large platter or basket for bread and a simple goblet or even a tumbler for wine will work well. Other useful dishes are small bowls that can be held in one hand for oils, and pitchers and large basins for baptismal renewal, foot-washing, or other cleansing rituals.

There is no reason to reserve these dishes and linens for holy use only. Holiness is not limited, but expansive, and the Holy One can be encountered anywhere in our lives, not only when we are doing our liturgical work together as a community, but also in the ordinariness of our living. However, there is a good reason to use the same things over and over again. In such use, the things themselves take on the memories of community celebrations and commemorations and become laden with the collective life of the community.

PRAYERS FOR HOLY THINGS

A PRAYER UPON SEEING A NATURAL BEAUTIFUL THING

(This prayer and the one following may be adapted for use by a group, if appropriate, by changing to plural pronouns. The specific thing for which thanks are given may be named, if desired.)

In this beautiful (thing),
I see your Wisdom at play, Holy One.
I am filled with wonder
at your creation.

A PRAYER UPON SEEING A BEAUTIFUL THING MADE BY HUMAN HANDS

Holy Wisdom,
you guide the hand, the eye, the imagination
that made this beautiful (thing).
Blessed are you, Holy One!
All our fresh springs are in you!

A PRAYER FOR GUIDANCE IN CHOOSING THINGS FOR LITURGY

With your Holy Wisdom,
guide our imagination.
With your Holy Spirit,
fill our minds and hearts.

Show us your beauty and usefulness
in this (thing).
Hallow it to our use
and bless us through it.

ℭ

A Prayer of Blessing for a Liturgical Object

*(This blessing can be adapted for use with devotional objects, liturgical
furnishings, or other items to be used for liturgical purposes. Although
such things are always hallowed by their use in a context of prayer, special
circumstances might recommend the use of such a blessing.)*

Holy One,
in the beginning you made all things
and called them Good.
Through Holy Wisdom, friend of humanity,
you call your beloved people to see and know you.
With the power of your Holy Spirit, who blows where she
     wills,
you fill all things with your presence.
In our use of this good (thing)
may we see you,
know you,
and be filled with your presence.

RESOURCES FOR HOLY THINGS

Dillard, Annie. *Pilgrim at Tinker Creek*. New York: HarperPerennial, 1998.

Elkins, Heather Murray. *Holy Stuff of Life: Stories, Poems, and Prayers about Human Things*. Cleveland: Pilgrim Press, 2006.

Kingsolver, Barbara. *Small Wonder: Essays*. New York: HarperCollins, 2002.

FIVE

BODIES

I praise you,
for I am fearfully and wonderfully made.

—Psalm 139:14

THINKING ABOUT BODIES

Human bodies are at once the *sine qua non* of any liturgy (how can we enact a liturgy without the presence of our bodies?) and at the same time the contested problem of Christian liturgy and theology. Much of the Christian spiritual tradition has emphasized subduing and disciplining one's body, viewing the human body as an enemy of the spirit. Women's bodies especially have been denied, rejected, and regarded with fear and suspicion as a source of contamination. This burdensome and harmful tradition is not limited to Christians, but is found among many of the world's religions. Moreover, popular Western culture glorifies a distorted and artificial ideal of the human body, both male and female. The disabled body, the nonwhite body, the gay or lesbian or transgendered body, the not-thin-enough body, the not-muscled-enough body, the not-fit-enough body, the not-stylish-enough body: these bodies all fail to meet the unrealistic cultural norms that dominate the Westernized world in which we live. At the same time, Christian religious traditions tend to regard all bodies, fit or unfit, stylish or not, as suspect, corrupt containers, at best, of the spiritual core of human beings. Feminist Christian spirituality aims to claim the God-given beauty of the human body, in all its rich variety, and to rejoice in the gifts of our human female bodies especially. Countering toxic cultural and religious attitudes toward bodies, feminist Christian spirituality affirms and celebrates human bodies as vehicles of divine grace. However, the power of cultural and religious messages cannot be denied and demands powerful ritual and spiritual disciplines as a resisting force.

We find one such resisting force hidden within the very language of worship. First, our English word "worship" comes from an old English word, *weorth-scipe*, meaning "worthiness." In its original context, it refers to something or someone to whom honor, respect, and esteem is due. So as we commonly use the word worship as a noun ("Sunday worship"), its original significance as representing an attitude, a disposition, is often lost. Worship is a verb, and to worship is to ascribe honor. Early English Bible translators used the word "worship" for the Hebrew word meaning "bow down," or "bow the head."

The Greek words usually translated as "worship" carry similar embodied meanings, especially *proskeuneo*, literally "to come forward to kiss the hand." So worship carries hidden within these twin gifts: to honor *with* the body (to bow down) and an honoring *of* the body (to kiss the hand).

This serves as a powerful reminder of the sheer physicality of worship: worship always involves the use of physical space, physical objects, and, above all, our irreducibly physical bodies. And notice carefully that this recognition of our bodies is not a grudging acknowledgment, but a whole-hearted rejoicing in our bodies: we honor the Holy with our holy bodies, we honor our holy and beautiful bodies. It is a strange thing indeed that the fact of our physicality is so deeply buried in mainstream understandings of worship.

A feminist emancipatory practice of honoring the body recognizes the blessing of diversity of bodies, the beauty and inviolability of every body, and the right and indeed necessity of every one to enjoy and value her or his own body and to respect and honor the bodies of others.

SPIRITUAL DISCIPLINES OF THE BODY

Spiritual disciplines involving the body include taking time to pay attention to our breathing, learning to center ourselves using this natural body rhythm, and also making the effort to care intentionally for our bodies.

A Spiritual Practice of Holy Breath

The breath is the spirit of the body, the *anima, ruach, spiritus*. This discipline connects us with the animating spirit that enlivens our bodies. It may be done alone or in a group, indoors or outdoors. If done indoors, open a window or door to admit some fresh air, if this is feasible. It is always best to wear loose-fitting, comfortable clothes that do not restrict movement. This discipline may be done barefoot, if desired. If this discipline is done with a group, it is probably advisable for one person to read the following instructions as the group goes through the movement. This discipline is valuable at the beginning of the day or at the beginning of a service, a gathering, or creative work. Depending on the context and needs, it may be done in silence or accompanied by quiet recorded music or humming. No words are necessary, and it may be most restful and renewing if undertaken in silence, making of one's breath and simple movement a wordless prayer.

Reclining version:

You will need a comfortable floor mat such as a yoga mat, futon, or padded rug for this version. Gently let yourself down onto the mat, first seated, then lower yourself onto your back. Stretch your legs out, slightly apart. Let the feet drop open. If this is uncomfortable for your lower back, place your feet on the floor, knees bent, heels slightly turned out to let the knees rest on each other for comfort and support. Let your arms extend slightly out from the body, with the palms facing up. You may want a rolled towel or very small pillow to cushion your head. Shoulders are back and down, chest open, neck long and relaxed. Roll the head gently from side to side until you find a comfortable place.

Close your eyes.

Breathe through the nose, in and out, drawing the breath up from the ground through your spine, releasing the breath gently into the air.

Breathing gently and regularly, feel the circle of your breath, from earth to heaven and back again. As you inhale, feel the air fill your belly, ribs, chest. As you exhale, feel your belly sink back toward your spine.

Notice how the ribs expand and fold like wings on each breath.

Let each inhale lengthen and deepen. When you have filled your body with air, let it out smoothly and naturally. As you empty yourself of air, rest a moment at the bottom of each breath. Then let the belly fill again, and continue until you are completely relaxed.

To bring this relaxation exercise to a close, roll onto your right side, knees drawn up and head resting on the right arm. After a few breaths, slowly raise yourself up with your arms into a comfortable seated position. Fold your hands at your breast in a prayer position for a moment, giving thanks for breath.

Standing version:

Stand with feet shoulder width apart, feet in full contact with the floor.

Spread the toes to grip the floor firmly. Knees are slightly flexed. Shoulders are back and down, chest open, neck long and relaxed.

Arms hang loosely from the shoulders, palms facing forward.

Breathe through the nose, in and out, drawing the breath up from the ground through the soles of the feet, releasing the breath gently through the top of the head.

Breathing gently and regularly, feel the circle of your breath, from earth to heaven and back again.

As you breathe, see how the ribs expand like wings on each breath.

With each breath, bring your body into balance, feet, legs, buttocks, stomach, chest, shoulders, neck, and head.

Feel the springiness of your body as it moves with each breath.

Breathe for one minute. If your balance is secure, you may want to close your eyes.

As you inhale, let your arms float upward, riding the breath, palms facing upward, until they meet over your head, or as far as is comfortable.

As your hands rise up over your head, your head will want to tilt upward, carried on the flow of your breath.

As you exhale, let your arms float down, palms facing downward, until they return to your sides. Your head will want to float down with your hands. Repeat three times.

At the conclusion of the third movement, draw the hands together at the breast in a prayer position. Give thanks for the gift of breath.

Seated version:

Sit on a straight chair, feet firmly and solidly placed on the floor shoulder width apart. Knees are bent at right angles, toes spread to rest on the floor.

Weight is balanced evenly on the pelvic bones, back rising upward from the bowl of the pelvis, shoulders down and back, neck long and relaxed.

Arms hang loosely from the shoulders.

Palms are resting lightly on the upper thighs.

Breathe through the nose, in and out, drawing the breath up from the ground through the feet, releasing the breath gently through the top of the head.

Breathing gently and regularly, feel the circle of your breath, from earth to heaven and back again.

As you breathe, notice how the ribs expand like wings on each breath.

With each breath, bring your body into balance, feet, legs, buttocks, stomach, chest, shoulders, neck, and head.

Feel the springiness of your body as it moves with each breath. Breathe for one minute. You may want to close your eyes.

As you inhale, let your arms float upward, riding the breath, palms facing upward, until they meet over your head, as far as you are comfortable.

As your hands rise up over your head, your head will want to tilt upward, carried on the flow of your breath.

As you exhale, let your arms float down, palms facing downward, until they return to your sides.

Your head will want to float down with your hands. Repeat three times.

At the conclusion of the third movement, draw the hands together at the breast in a prayer position. Give thanks for the gift of breath.

A Spiritual Practice of Care of One's Body

Bodies vary in shape, ability, and general health. We not only worship with and in our bodies, our ritual practices are grounded in a physical, material life of eating, washing, working, and so on. In order to perceive the deep interconnections between liturgy and life, a spiritual practice that honors the body's particular beauty will attend to three things:

1. *Nourishment:* Food that supplies basic nutritional needs will also foster respect for one's body. Food that is fresh, whole, and prepared with love and eaten with attention will also nourish the spirit. Approach food with joy and gratitude!

2. *Rest:* Care of the body includes rest and relaxation. Adequate sleep and relaxing activities are important aspects of preparing to worship. Rest should include regular disciplines of meditation, reflection, or prayer, when both mind and body are relaxed but alert.

3. *Activity:* To balance the need for rest, it is important also to engage in a regular discipline of physical activity, appropriate to one's physical abilities and inclinations. This might take the form of gardening, yoga, or tai chi, as well as some more conventional form of regular exercise.

BODY POSTURES, GESTURES AND VESTURE FOR WORSHIP

Traditional postures, gestures, and vesture for Christian worship and prayer are drawn chiefly from the Roman civil and imperial ceremonial for approaching rulers and social superiors in a patriarchal and hierarchical society. Thus the actions of bowing the head, clasping the hands in petition, kneeling, and prostrating oneself on the floor are all gestures intended to convey submission to a higher authority, whether judge, king, bishop, or God. Traditional vestments, likewise, are adapted from imperial dress of royal ceremonial, with signs of office and status. While we may find that on occasion such gestures and postures express the suitable attitude, it is important to be aware of the history of these gestures and the ways in which they can subtly form us for submission.

If we did not conceive of God as an all-powerful potentate, how would we approach the Holy One? By what gestures would we be known? How would we vest ourselves? The development of appropriate postures, gestures, vestments, and movements must take place in your own specific context. Following are some basics to keep in mind when planning liturgies.

Begin with the bodies

Often when planning liturgies we attend first to the words that will be said, only later (if at all) giving thought to the placement and movement and attitudes of the bodies that will say and hear and respond to the words. Instead, ask what posture is the aim of the liturgy, then what gestures or movement will place the bodies in that posture. For example, if the liturgy is a joyous event, the desired posture is one expressive of joy. Depending on the context, this might include dancing, clapping, holding hands or embracing, lifting the hands up, shaking the hands, and so on. If the liturgy is reflective or meditative, slow gestures, quiet postures, and little if any movement is appropriate. Ask yourself: what does the body know about this event? This is especially important when planning baptism and meal liturgies, in which the center of the rite is the human bodies being washed and being fed. Let what the body knows about washing and about eating guide your planning. Above all, do not let the words of these liturgies take priority over the presence of the bodies.

Let the bodies move

So much of conventional Christian worship is static and stationary that we often forget that Christianity was a movement before it was a religion. Reclaim the "Christian movement" by arranging the space for the community to move about.

One ancient and very powerful but simple movement is the procession. Basically a procession is a group of people moving from one place to another. By creating two or more worship sites (traditionally called "stations"), the community can move from one to the next. For example, the portion of the liturgy focused on reading and speaking (often called "the liturgy of the Word") might take place in a space suited for sitting and hearing. The portion of the liturgy focused on a communal action such as a meal (eucharistic or otherwise) might appropriately take place in a space more suited to gathering around a table. Processions can also move a group through a particular community as a form of witness. The ancient Stations of the Cross can have just such a purpose when enacted in public spaces.

Even movement in place such as swaying to music, lifting hands, facing in different directions, holding hands or linking arms can be very powerful.

Encourage comfortable dress for worshipers and leaders

The joy and power of physical movement is limited by constricting forms of dress. Comfortable clothing that permits movement will encourage physical participation, and a sense of celebration should be encouraged for all who attend. Presiders (whether lay or ordained) should wear some garment that readily identifies them as leaders. It helps participants to engage in the liturgy if they can easily identify its leaders, especially if leadership varies by choice or necessity. Presiders' garments should, in addition to serving as a means of identification, be both beautiful and functional. Some forms of traditional presiders' garments are uncomfortable as well as historically male forms of dress. The ancient forms of the chasuble and cope, however, were outer garments worn by both men and women. A simple poncho-type or cape-type garment can serve well for presiders while leaving room to move. Such garments may be made simply out of lightweight and beautiful fabric, with or without embellishments. One community attaches small bells to the hem of these garments, adding music to the movement of leaders. Presiders especially should make it a point to wear comfortable shoes that allow graceful movement and that don't make loud noises when walking. Sensible shoes are an important element in establishing natural and relaxed posture and lend confidence to one's presiding.

Posture and gesture should be natural and simple

When clothing is simple and comfortable, permitting full range of movement, and when attention is given to the use of bodies in ways that are appropriate for the event, gestures will flow naturally. The size of gestures should be scaled to the size of the community: the larger the group, the larger the gesture. But all gestures of presiders should be clear and open, conveying both confidence and invitation.

Consider these basic patterns of movement when planning a liturgy

1. *Procession:* This need not be as regimented as a parade. It is simply a way of moving people from one place to another. If the event is celebrative, the movement may be accompanied by music or musical sounds (bells, chimes, rattles, drums, etc.) and may include informal dancing movements. If it is a meditative or penitential event, a silent procession is very powerful. If the event is a lament, wailing and unmusical sounds (unpitched drums and rattles and the like) can be a way of expressing anguish and outrage. If the aim of the liturgy is to move the participants, emotionally, spiritually, or intellectually, incorporating physical movement from one place to another can be a very effective nonverbal means of doing so. Movement of the community into and away from the gathering space for worship, movement to and from the communion table or baptismal font—all can be seen as processions and enjoyed as such.

2. *Circle dance:* An open space or adequate aisle space is required for this to work effectively. A central focal point, such as a communion table or baptismal font, is desirable. The community may simply walk in a circle holding hands or placing hands on shoulders, or a more structured dance step can be used. A simple grapevine step is one example, where dancers step one foot in front and then the next in back, moving to the side. Music or a simple drumbeat will help the circle stay in step. The tempo can be quick for a celebrative event, or slow for a more stately movement.

3. *Spiral dance:* Similar to the circle dance, the spiral dance best begins as a circle, which then opens when one person drops the hand of one person and turns the circle inward on itself. This is a more complex form than the circle dance, and requires some practice, at least on the part of a few of the presiders, who can then lead the rest of the group. It also requires more open space than the circle dance, since a central focal point is soon lost sight of when the spiral unwinds. With a large group, it works well outdoors. It can also be an effective concluding dance, leading out and away from the gathering space as a kind of danced dismissal. As with the circle dance, rhythmic music will help keep the group together. A remarkable fourteenth-century Italian fresco shows a group of women engaged in a complex spiral dance, accompanied by a single drummer with a small hand drum. The women are grave and solemn, linking little fingers very lightly, and taking small steps.

Consider these basic postures and gestures when planning a liturgy

1. *Standing prayer:* The most ancient prayer posture of Christians and Jews is standing. A posture of standing emphasizes our equality with one another and our dignity before the Holy One. It fosters courage and models the power to "stand up for ourselves."

2. *Seated prayer:* This posture is best suited to listening activities, whether listening to God in meditative prayer, listening to readers and preachers speak to us, or listening to and speaking with one another. This posture encourages mutual respect and thoughtful reflection.

3. *Orans position:* This is a graceful gesture of hands raised to shoulder level, palm facing up while standing. A gesture common in the ancient world, as seen on frescoes, mosaics, and manuscripts, it expresses openness and offering. It may be used during prayer by the whole community or by the leader as an invitation to join in prayer. The arms are not held stiffly by the sides, but extended generously away in a smooth upward movement, the chest and face lifting at the same time.

4. *Prayer position:* The classical prayer position, palms together, hands at heart, is a traditional gesture of petition. It also functions at times as a centering gesture. In a more emotive form of this gesture the hands are clasped together and may be raised up in entreaty.

5. *Bows:* Bows ranging from the simple nod of the head to a profound bow bending from the waist have traditionally indicated subservience. However, in some contexts a bow, mutually exchanged, can be a powerful way of honoring one another in the body. A simple bow of the head can be combined with mutual handclasp for a gesture of greeting and respect.

6. *Kiss of peace:* One of the most ancient Christian gestures, the kiss of peace was originally a full kiss on the lips, as a sign of the mutual trust and love between Christians (see Rom. 16:16, 1 Cor. 16:20, 2 Cor. 13:12, 1 Thes. 5:26). In subsequent centuries it became clericalized to the point that only clergy exchanged the kiss, and it eventually dropped out of use altogether. It is a gesture that expresses a higher degree of comfort with the body than most of us enjoy in these times, and should be used judiciously and only after prayerful consideration. A less threatening gesture such as a kiss on each cheek or a clasping of hands and a mutual bow may be appropriate modifications.

Modify these gestures as appropriate

It is important to invite modifications of any gestures or movements for those who are not comfortable with them or who have mobility disabilities. Explicit invitation to the participants to modify should be made as part of every liturgy. No coercion should ever be used where bodily movement and gesture is concerned. Full respect for the bodily integrity of all participants is essential.

Make space for those who do not wish to engage in the more complex movements

Some may prefer to participate more passively in movements such as the circle dance, spiral dance, or procession. Leaving literal space in the room, providing seating for those who need to sit, and finding other ways for them to participate, such as tapping a drum or other instrument, can embody Wisdom's house that welcomes all.

PRAYERS FOR THE BODY

A BREATHING PRAYER

(This prayer may be used by an individual or a group—replacing "I" with "we"—as a concluding prayer to the spiritual practice of breathing outlined previously. Or it may be used as a breath practice itself, prayed slowly with a full breath between each line.)

Holy Spirit, Breath of God
for this breath I give thanks
for this breath I give praise
with this breath I know peace
with this breath I know wonder
with this breath I know you.

A LITANY OF PRAISE FOR THE BODY

(This prayer may be used by an individual or a group—replacing "I" with "we." In either case, the optional gestures may be performed by each individual, as she or he chooses. This litany may form part of an event celebrating life cycle events of the body, such as first menses, monthly menstruation, or menopause, or simply an occasion such as Holy Body Day.)

It was you who formed my inward parts;
you knit me together in my mother's womb.
I praise you, for I am fearfully and wonderfully made.

(Clasping hands together firmly)
For sinew and bone
for muscle and nerve,
we praise you,
for we are fearfully and wonderfully made!

(Placing hands on head)
For skull and brain
and flashing thought,
we praise you,
for we are fearfully and wonderfully made!

(Placing hands on heart)
For pumping heart
and blood and breath,
we praise you,
for we are fearfully and wonderfully made!

(Extending hands, palms up:)
For clever hands
(Stepping lightly in place or tapping feet on the floor)
and grounded feet,
we praise you,
for we are fearfully and wonderfully made!

(Wrapping arms around the body)
For all parts hidden and lovely,
necessary and beloved,
we praise you,
for we are fearfully and wonderfully made!

Wonderful are your works;
that I know very well.
My frame was not hidden from you,
when I was being made in secret,
intricately woven in the depths of the earth.
We praise you,
for we are fearfully and wonderfully made!

☾

A PRAYER FOR A CIRCLE DANCE[12]

(The community joins hands in a circle. A leader stands in the center of the circle, calling out the litany as the group responds while dancing or walking in a circle. This is best if it is sung to a very simple chant or tune, at the leader's discretion. A light rhythm may be kept on a small drum or other rhythm instrument. If desired, the drummer may stand in the center with the leader, or the leader may be the drummer. The leader's words may be abbreviated, expanded, or improvised as desired.)

Answer "Amen" to me! Glory be to you, Holy One!

Amen!

Glory be to you, Wisdom! Glory be to your Holy Word!

Amen!

Glory be to you, Spirit! Glory be to your power and grace!

Amen!

We praise you, Holy One, source of light and darkness!

Amen!

We give you thanks, for all things have their beginning and
    their end in you!

Amen!

I will be saved and I will save!

Amen!

I will be loosed and I will loose!

Amen!

I will be wounded, and I will wound!

Amen!

I will be born, and I will bear!

Amen!

I will eat, and I will be eaten!

Amen!

I will hear, and I will be heard!

Amen!

I will be washed, and I will wash!

Amen!

I will pipe; dance, all of you!
Amen!
I will mourn; beat you all your breasts!
Amen!
Holy Wisdom sings praises with us!
Amen!
The Holy Spirit dances on high!
Amen!
To the universe belongs the dancer!
Amen!
To the dancer belongs the wisdom of the universe!
Amen!
Amen!

Suggestions for a Spiral Dance

1. Musicians and drummers should be prepared with appropriate music to help lead the movement. When a group is first learning this movement, it is well to keep the music somewhat slow and measured, with a simple, steady beat. In a complex movement like a spiral dance, it is often best not to require that the dancers also sing.

2. Not everyone must dance in order to enjoy the dance. Invite nondancers to serve as singers or musicians.

3. This movement requires a large open space, even for a modest size group. The floor or ground should be cleared of any obstacles that might cause someone to stumble.

4. Begin with everyone who wishes to dance in a circle, facing outward, holding hands lightly or linking little fingers. If the group is large, form two or more concentric circles.

5. When the music begins, the circle begins to turn counterclockwise, slowly. When it has made at least one complete circuit, one dancer (designated beforehand) drops the hand of the person on her left and turns in to face the person on her right, moving clockwise. The rest of the line follows the first dancer, moving clockwise and unwinding the circle. The first dancer leads the line into a spiral, moving toward the center of the dancing circle, all facing into the center. The first dancer then turns again to move counterclockwise, again unwinding the spiral, moving outward and leading the dancers outward until the spiral is completely unwound and the circle restored. The first dancer may then join hands with the person on her left to complete the circle. This pattern can be repeated as desired.

6. The best music for this kind of dance is simple and repetitive, so that it can be repeated and elaborated upon until the dance is complete. As a group becomes more familiar with the dance, music that increases in tempo can be used, so that the dance begins slowly but gradually grows in intensity.

Suggestions for Observing Holy Body Day

"What do you need for a holiday? A date, a legend, a blessing, and a meal."[11]

First suggested in Esther Broner's novel, A Weave of Women, Holy Body Day can be observed by a small group of women or a small mixed group of women, men, and children. The shape of the celebration should be adapted to meet the needs and desires of the group, but might include:

1. Bathing in scented water or massage with scented oil; anointing one another's face or hands or feet with oil.

2. The use of scented candles or incense.

3. Music, either recorded or created by the group, that is calming and renewing.

4. Creation of a gathering space that emphasizes beauty and comfort, including pillows, rugs, and comfortable seating.

5. A full meal or light food that is simple, refreshing, and somewhat indulgent (not an occasion to count calories, but with due attention to any health-related dietary restrictions). Each participant might bring a dish to share that emphasizes pleasure and comfort.

6. Prayers of thanksgiving for the body and its senses, as good gifts of the Holy One and a sign of the work of Wisdom.

7. Telling of stories that emphasize the goodness of our bodies and senses: beautiful things seen, heard, felt, eaten, and so forth.

RESOURCES FOR THE BODY

Eiesland, Nancy. *The Disabled God: Toward a Liberatory Theology of Disability*. Nashville: Abingdon Press, 1994.

Eiesland, Nancy, and Don Saliers, eds. *Human Disability and the Service of God: Reassessing Religious Practice*. Nashville: Abingdon Press, 1998.

Isherwood, Lisa, and Elizabeth Stuart. *Introducing Body Theology*. Sheffield, England: Sheffield Academic Press, 1998.

Moltmann-Wendel, Elisabeth. *I Am My Body: A Theology of Embodiment*. Translated by John Bowden. New York: Continuum, 1995.

Paulsell, Stephanie. *Honoring the Body: Meditations on a Christian Practice*. San Francisco: Jossey-Bass, 2002.

Schroeder, Celeste. *Embodied Prayer: Harmonizing Body and Soul*. Liguori, Mo.: Triumph Press, 1995.

Tufnell, Miranda, and Chris Crickmay. *Body Space Image: Notes towards Improvisation and Performance*. London: Dance Books Ltd., 1993.

SIX

SOUND

Let the sea roar, and all that fills it;
The world and all those who live in it.
Let the floods clap their hands,
Let the hills sing together for joy at the presence of the Holy One.

—Psalm 98:7–9

THINKING ABOUT SOUND

Sound and its partner, silence, give shape and significance to time. It might be said that patterns of sounds and silences are in fact one of our primary means of speaking the language of "time." Indeed, sound and silence occur only in time and live only in memory. From the memory of sound we make marks that remind us of the sounds that were made. When we play a recording, we are hearing the memory of sounds that took place in the past.

When we think of sound in liturgy and worship, we normally think of music. But consider the sounds that also are part of any worship service: voices speaking, singing, weeping, and shouting, hands clapping, feet tapping or shuffling on the floor, paper rustling, books being moved about, perhaps bells ringing or chimes sounding, people whispering and moving about, clothing rustling, chairs being moved, babies crying, children fussing, fans humming or fire snapping, cars driving by, sirens sounding, trains rattling or whistling, voices outside shouting, and so on. The list is long, varied, and contextual.

There are many books and articles on the subject of music in worship, and some of these are found in the list of resources at this chapter's end. Here we will consider the use of sound in the broader sense, not limited to tonal music—hymns, songs, anthems, and the like—but percussive rhythm, nonverbal vocal sounds, and silence. All of these are part of the vocabulary of sounds that we rarely consider when we think of worship services, but they have much power in themselves and, well used, can engage worshipers on a deep level.

Sound and Silence

Consider how the sound of the human voice is manufactured: air is taken in and expelled across the vocal chords, causing them to vibrate. The sound thus produced is then given shape by the mouth, tongue, and lips. In order to speak or sing, we must first breathe. And our breath is itself both a gift of the Holy One ("and breathed into [them] the breath of life," Gen. 2:7) and a sign of the presence of the Holy Spirit of God ("a sound like the rush of a violent wind," Acts 2:2).

Each time we draw breath, we re-enact our creation in the image of God; each time we speak, we re-embody the giving of the gift of the Holy Spirit.

Consider silence: absolute silence does not exist in the world of the living. But by ceasing to speak, by assuming a listening and attentive stance, we begin to notice the small sounds around us and within us: the sound of our own breath, our heartbeat drumming softly, the blood moving through our body; the sounds made by other living beings, whether other humans or other creatures with whom we share the planet. It is in silence that we begin to experience our connectedness to all that is and to all that exists not only in our presence but also beyond it. The psalmist says that nature itself is animated and declares praise to God in its own language: seas roar, floods clap, and hills sing. So when we roar and clap our hands and sing, we add our voices and bodies and breath to a sound of praise that is already in progress, this remarkable cacophony that rises to heaven and shakes the ground.

If sound is complex and rich, mingling human voices with those of an animate universe, silence is much more than the absence of sound. It can be experienced as the absence of God, and the cry of lament is a call to the Holy One to break silence and to speak to us in our distress: "You have seen; do not be silent!" (Ps. 35:22). For humans, silence equals death, where the noisy sound of praise is not heard, the tremor of sound does not reverberate. In life, silence can equal death, when we keep silence in the face of inhumanity or injustice or greed, and the result can be death of the soul (of those who keep silent as well as those who suffer directly) as well as real physical death—the deaths of the poor, the oppressed, the nonhuman world of plants and animals, water and air. "While I kept silence, my body wasted away" (Ps. 32:3). To keep silence in the face of such suffering and loss is to enter into death, from which no cry of praise arises. And to be silenced is to die another kind of death, the death of one's voice, one's presence in the world: "Let a woman learn in silence with full submission. I permit no woman to teach or to have authority over a man; she is to keep silent" (1 Tim. 2:11–12). "Don't ask, don't tell." "Children should be seen and not heard." "Don't speak unless you are spoken to."

In the face of this deathly silence, the clamor of praise is also the clamor of protest, the lifting up of voices—human, animal, plant, water, and sky—to claim their voices and the power of life. Wisdom "calls from the highest places in the town." To make noise is to be alive. And a person, a world, a universe fully alive is praise to the Holy One, the Living One.

But there is also silence that is full, and not empty, rich with presence rather than echoing of absence. This full silence is heard in a listening, attentive quiet that allows the still small voice to be heard, as in the prophet Elijah's encounter with the Holy One:

> Now there was a great wind, so strong that it was splitting the mountains and breaking rocks in pieces before the Holy One, but the Holy One was not in the wind; and after the wind an earthquake, but the Holy One was not in the earthquake; and after the earthquake a fire, but the Holy One was not in the fire; and after the fire a sound of sheer silence. (1 Kings 19:11–12)

This silence is full of the presence of the Holy One, who speaks in the stillness, the letting go that makes silence possible, and the attention that fills it with presence: "Be still, and know that I am God" (Ps. 46:10).

Sound and silence, noise and stillness are sisters, partners in the worship of the Holy One.

On Finding Your Own Voice and Hearing Voices of Others

Essential to the process of making room for full silence and lively sound is finding your own voice. As individuals we are often discouraged, for a variety of reasons, from developing and loving our own voices. As groups—especially groups with a history of suppression and repression—we need to give voice to the cries of our hearts, the joys and the sorrows, the rages and the celebrations, as a necessary part of our emancipatory process. There are more and more publications of songs and music that give expression to these cries, that put word and music together in ways that we can all join in together, either in celebrating or lamenting our own stories or in empathetic celebration or lament with others. A Christian emancipatory community will want to have a collection of the best of these for regular use in worship. A select list of such resources is included in the next section and at the end of this chapter, but each community will add to this list as new resources are discovered.

Equally important is making room for creative voices within the community to contribute music, poetry, prayers, meditations, and other writings that can help the community find its own voice. Encourage the poets, writers, and musicians among you! But it is important to balance the creative work that comes from within the community with creative work that comes from other communities. For other individuals and communities represent voices and experiences that expand the community's vocabulary of praise and lament and enable the community to transcend its own limitations and to pray in solidarity with others whose experiences differ.

A SPIRITUAL DISCIPLINE OF SOUND AND SILENCE

Spiritual practices of sound and silence intend to help us experience the varieties of both sound and silence in the world, to attend to and learn from these, and to explore their presence in worship. As with learning to attend to holy things, we take three steps: first, slow down and still the body, the breath, and the mind. Second, reduce what we can call aural clutter, finding a place that is quiet, shutting off as much of the unnecessary noise and clatter as possible. And third, focus attention and open ourselves to silence, then to the sounds around us and within us, and finally to make our own sounds with intention. Let us explore each step with care.

1. *Slow down.* Sit or stand in a relaxed position, spine straight and open, chest up and out to make plenty of room for breathing, ribcage expanding with each breath. Let the breath fill the ribcage all the way down to the pelvis, pushing the bellybutton out with each intake of breath. Release the breath so that the belly sinks back into the spine. Listen to your breath. Breathe in through the nose, out through the mouth. Listen to your heartbeat. Hear the rhythm of your body.

2. *Let the quiet speak.* Now listen to the sounds outside your own body. What do you hear? What sounds or vibrations do you become aware of within the quiet? What is it telling you?

3. *Focus and express.* Let your breath direct your body, by tapping your fingers or feet to the sound of your breath or to the beat of your heart. Let the tapping become clapping of your hands, stamping of your feet. Let your breath come with energy, with a sigh. Give the breath a rhythm. Let a sound come out of your body, not a vocalized sound, not yet a word, just a sound that is attuned with the sound inside and outside your body. Listen to yourself within the sound of the universe. Listen to the wind of the Spirit moving through you and in you. Give thanks for the gift of the Spirit.

PATTERNS: A Vocabulary of Sound for Worship

Music, silence, and the rhythm of the spoken word are often treated as secondary elements to be added after the content of a liturgy has been determined. But what if we think of sound and silence as integral elements of liturgy, to be planned at the same time that one plans the verbal and physical content of an event? Like bodies in worship, sound and silence are also foundational, and without them rituals of worship could not take place. Following are some things to keep in mind when planning a service.

All speech is first of all sound and silence

Be aware of the rhythm of spoken words, whether in prayers, scripture or other readings, or any other liturgical speech. Some sense of rhythm is found in the sounds of the words themselves; sometimes it is found in the context and meaning. Consider this when writing or preparing any spoken words. When writing text to be read in unison, keep it brief and repetitive. This enhances the rhythmic power of group speaking and enables those who don't read to participate in the simple repeated text. Give longer verbal texts to single voices.

All speech and song is breath (Spirit)

Every word spoken or sung in a service is a potential avenue for the working of the Holy Spirit. Therefore, care must be taken with every word. Words should never be spoken carelessly or thoughtlessly.

Respect the need for silence

All speech requires silence, whether the briefest silences between words and sentences, or longer and more intentionally focused periods of silence. Like speech, silence requires careful preparation and thoughtful leadership. When preparing spoken texts, plan the silences as carefully as the spoken text.

Let the silences be full of presence

This can be encouraged by careful and intentional use of words and music and nonmusical sound, as well as by thoughtful placement of periods of silence and intentional leadership of silence. Full silences can take place with the whole community seated and still together or with movement. Make the silence meaningful by using it to emphasize spoken text or action or to provide time for meditation on a text, action, or object.

Foster the use of a full range of sounds

Where appropriate, consider encouraging the community to express themselves vocally with sighs, moans or other voiced laments, or with shouts, cries, and laughter of joy and celebration. The psalms are an excellent place to begin experiencing these expressions, since the psalmist often invokes such expressions as "shout for joy," or "I cry out to you," or "my tears have been my food." Likewise, the use of nonmusical sounds such as clapping, stamping, drumming, or making use of rattles or other noisemaking instruments can also increase the sound vocabulary of a community. If you are fortunate to have trained musicians who can lead drumming or other simple rhythmic action in worship, you are blessed. But you need not let the lack of someone who is trained prevent the community from trying this. Keep it simple and encourage everyone, especially children in the community, to try it. A joyful noise (or a sorrowful noise) need not be musically sophisticated in order to be effective and powerful.

Link sounds with liturgical texts

Use a small hand drum to accompany readings, where appropriate, or during portions of the eucharistic prayer, or while people are moving about engaged in some congregational liturgical activity, such as receiving communion or anointing one another, or the like. A bell tree, wind chime, or other bell-like instrument can also be used to punctuate or accompany readings, prayers, or liturgical action. Music, either instrumental or sung, is especially powerful as support for liturgical action. Processions or movement forward of any kind benefit from music. If processional music is sung, the text is best kept very simple and repetitive, so that movement is not hampered by having to handle books or printed texts. The music should be chosen to enhance and strengthen the liturgical action. If the context is celebratory, the music should reflect and intensify that experience. If the liturgy is solemn, or meditative, quiet music can invite quiet movement.

Link form of music with the context

Some sung music, especially hymns, is best used when the community is focused on the act of singing itself. Stanza hymns, with complex ideas and progression of concepts through a series of stanzas, demand full attention while singing. Cyclic or repetitious songs, such as the music associated with worship at Taizè, France, or *coritos* of Hispanic music, serve best as part of ritual action or as an element of meditation. These songs work best when repeated frequently so that all present may learn to participate without having to refer to printed texts or music. This frees worshipers for movement, ritual actions, or deep contemplation.

Patterns: Some Suggested Hymns

Each community will want to create its own list of useful hymns, either out of its own denomination hymnal or from a variety of resources. Remember that all hymn *texts, music, and arrangements* are covered by copyright law, often independently of each other. Publication of any copyrighted material—hymn text, hymn tune, or hymn arrangement—in any place, whether a bulletin, projection slide, or a recording, requires permission from the copyright holder. This can be most easily done by obtaining a license from a copyright permission group, such as CCLI (http://www.ccli.com).

Denominational hymnals are always in the process of change. Such hymnals can be a valuable resource when used thoughtfully and intentionally. Members of the community will want to study hymn texts and tunes for suitableness to the community, the context, and the occasion. But because denominational hymnals take a long time to produce, they are, in some sense, out of date by the time they are published. New hymns are being written and published all the time, and new hymn writers are constantly emerging. Perhaps you have some in your community! Often a hymnal supplement or a trial hymnal will contain newer hymns and song, and newer hymnals and hymn collections also tend to take more care with the use of inclusive, emancipatory, and expansive language.

Here are some suggestions for feminist emancipatory hymns from a few mainline denominational hymnals. This is an idiosyncratic list, reflecting my interests, criteria, and preferences. For example, I have avoided hymns that use the terms "Lord" and included hymns that use "Father" to speak of the Holy One only if it is balanced by the use of female terms. Develop your own criteria and create your own list! Additional resources for hymns can be found at the end of this chapter.

The United Methodist Hymnal[13]

Hymns and canticles:
68: When in our music God is glorified
81: Canta, Debora, canta
87: What gift can we bring
88: Maker in whom we live
94: Praise God from whom all blessings flow
97: For the fruits of this creation
105: God of many names
109: Creating God, your fingers trace
111: How can we name a love
112: Canticle of Wisdom
113: Source and sovereign, rock and cloud
114: Many gifts, one Spirit
115: How like a gentle Spirit
118: The care the eagle gives her young
120: Your love, O God, is broad like beach and meadow
122: God of the sparrow, God of the whale
134: O Mary, don't you weep
143: On eagle's wings
145: Morning has broken
148: Many and great
150: God who stretched the spangled heavens
151: God created heaven and earth
164: Come my way, my truth, my life
192: There's a spirit in the air
194: Morning glory, starlit sky
198: My soul gives glory to my God

200: Tell out, my soul
202: People, look east
211: O come, O come, Emmanuel
233: En el frio invernal
263: When Jesus the healer
264: Silence, frenzied, unclean spirit
265: O Christ the healer
274: Woman in the night
276: The first one ever
305: Camina, pueblo de Dios
307: Christ is risen
309: On the day of resurrection
318: Christ is alive
330: Daw-Kee, Aim Daw-Tsi-Taw
331: Holy Spirit, come, confirm us
383: This is a day of new beginnings
406: Canticle of prayer
408: The gift of love
428: For the healing of the nations
432: Jesu, Jesu
434: Cuando el pobre
443: O God who shaped creation
478: Jaya ho
505: When our confidence is shaken
506: Wellspring of Wisdom
538: Wind who makes all winds that blow
543: O breath of life
544: Like the murmur of the dove's song
583: Sois la semilla
605: Wash, O God, your sons and daughters [baptism]
609: You have put on Christ [baptism]
610: We know that Christ is raised [baptism]
628: Eat this bread [eucharist]
637: Una espiga [eucharist]
646: Canticle of love
665: Go now in peace
666: Shalom to you

707: Hymn of Promise
725: Arise, shine out

Prayer responses:
72: Gloria
78: Heleluyan
486: Alleluia
487: This is our prayer
490: Hear us, O God

The Presbyterian Hymnal: Hymns, Psalms, and Spiritual Songs[14]

30: Born in the night, Mary's child
72: When Jesus came to Jordan
105: Because you live, O Christ
114/115: Come ye faithful, raise the strain
116: O sons and daughters, let us sing
128: On Pentecost they gathered
135: God is on, unique and holy
266: Thank you, God, for water, soil, and air
274: O God of earth and space
279: God of our growing years
285: God, you spin the whirling planets
287: God folds the mountains out of rock
300: Down to earth, as a dove
319: Spirit
320: The lone, wild bird
323: Loving Spirit
330: Deep in the shadows of the past
332: Live into hope
335: Though I may speak
343: Called as partners in Christ's service
348: Christian women, Christian men
349: Let all who pray the prayer Christ taught
385: O God, we bear the imprint of your face
386: O for a world
432: Canto de esperanza
433: There's a spirit in the air

471: O praise the gracious power
494: Out of deep, unordered water [baptism]
499: Wonder of wonder, here revealed [baptism]
514: Let us talents and tongues employ [eucharist]
515: Now to your table spread [eucharist]
547: Awit sa dapit hapon/When twilight comes
552: Give thanks, O Christian people
553: For the fruit of all creation

Renewing Worship Volume 5: New Hymns and Song[15]

102: Keep your lamps trimmed and burning
108: Unexpected and mysterious
124: Light shone in darkness
127: Christ, be our light
129: Bless now, O God, the journey
145: The risen Christ
153: Send down the fire
158: Crashing waters at creation [baptism]
160: Song over the waters [baptism]
162: Remember and rejoice [baptism]
166: As rain from the clouds
168: By your hand you feed your people [eucharist]
171: Seed that in earth is dying [eucharist]
172: Welcome table [eucharist]
175: United at the table/Unidos en la fiesta [eucharist]
176: Holy holy holy/Santo santo santo [eucharist]
178: Let us go now to the banquet/Vamos todos al banquete [eucharist]
181: All who hunger, gather gladly [eucharist]
184: What is this place
185: You are holy
188: The trees of the field
191: Rise, O church, like Christ arisen
193: Joyous light of heavenly glory
194: Now it is evening
212: Behold how pleasant/Miren que bueno
213: Although I speak with angel's tongues
216: Bring many names

218: Behold, God's chosen
219: All are welcome
220: Will you let me be your servant
225: Heaven is singing for joy/El cielo canta alegria
235: In deepest night
238: How long, O God
241: A place at the table
245: Canticle of the turning
246: When our song says peace
250: Light dawns on a weary world
253: When at last the rain falls/Al caer la lluvia
254: Touch the earth lightly
255: God the sculptor of the mountain
263: Calm to the waves
270: When memory fades
276: Will you come and follow me
283: Holy woman, graceful giver
289: Sing out, earth and skies
294: Praise the one who breaks the darkness

New Century Hymnal[16]

15: My heart is overflowing
20: God of Abraham and Moses
30: Colorful Creator
33: God created heaven and earth
36: To God compose a song of joy
41: I thank you, Jesus
57: O Holy Spirit, root of life
58: Spirit of love
62: Come, share the Spirit
73: Enter, rejoice, and come in
109: With joy draw water
118: Of the Parent's heart begotten
123: Mary woman of the promise
150: Sing a different song
151: 'Twas in the moon of wintertime
152: Born in the night, Mary's child

153: Who would think that that was what was needed
169: What ruler wades through murky streams
179: We yearn, O Christ, for wholeness
180: Blessed are the poor in spirit
196: When, like the woman at the well
206: A woman came who did not count the cost
231: Because you live, O Christ
236: Halleluja
272: On Pentecost they gathered
273: Praise with joy the world's creator
274: Womb of life and source of being
286: Spirit, Spirit of gentleness
291: O God, the Creator
335: Come, gather in this special place [eucharist]
340: Somos pueblo que camina/We are people on a journey [eucharist]
343: Jesus took the bread [eucharist]
344: The time was early evening [eucharist]
351: I was there to hear your borning cry
389: Un mandamiento nuevo
398: Shadow and substance
399: When minds and bodies meet as one
402: De colores
406: Not with naked eye
437: We shall not give up the fight
464: The weaver's shuttle swiftly flies
467: Mothering God, you gave me birth
468: The care the eagle gives her young
470: Golden breaks the dawn
501: We are dancing Sarah's circle
515: O God, my God
521: In solitude
526: Siyahamba/We are marching
554: Out of the depths, O God, we call
557: Pray for the wilderness
560: By whatever name we call you
564: We are not our own
575: O for a world

581: Lead us from death to life
583: Like a mother who has borne us
586: Come to tend God's garden
587: Through all the world, a hungry Christ
588: Let justice flow like streams

PRAYERS FOR SOUND AND SILENCE

A PRAYER WITHOUT WORDS

(This may be done alone or in a group.)

Breathe.

Listen.

Tap or drum in rhythm with your heartbeat.

Hum.

Listen.

Give thanks with breath and body sounds.

A PRAYER WITH WORDS AND SOUNDS

(One person speaks the prayer. Another person or several persons support the prayer with nonverbal sounds: sighs, moans, cries, clapping, stamping, drumming, sounding rhythm instruments, and ringing bells.)

(Begin softly, whispering)

Hear us, Holy One.

We listen for you.

We lift our hearts and our hands and our breath to you.

Hear us.

We listen for you.

(Silence)

(Louder)

Hear us, Holy One.

We hear you.

We lift our hearts and our hands and our breath to you.

Hear us!

We hear you!

(Clapping, drumming, sounding continues until it is done)

Amen.

A Prayer of Thanksgiving for the Gift of Music

Blessed are you, Holy One,
for you have put songs in our hearts
that we may praise you with our voices.
May our music give you glory
and may our lives be songs of praise to you
and to our Wisdom Jesus Christ.

RESOURCES FOR SOUND
Books

Bell, John L. *The Singing Thing Too: Enabling Congregations to Sing.* Glasgow: Wild Goose Publications, 2007.

Hernandez, Ana. *The Sacred Art of Chant: Preparing to Practice.* Woodstock, Vt.: Skylight Paths Publishing, 2005.

Hawn, C. Michael. *One Bread, One Body: Exploring Cultural Diversity in Worship.* Bethesda, Md.: Alban Institute, 2003.

Hymns and Songs

Aldredge-Clanton, Jann. *Inclusive Hymns for Liberating Christians.* Austin, Tex.: Eakin Press, 2006.

Bell, John L. *Seven Songs of Mary.* Glasgow: Wild Goose Publishing, 1998.

Bell, John, and Graham Maule. *Love and Anger: Songs of Lively Faith and Social Justice.* Glasgow: Wild Goose Publishing, 1997.

Bringle, Mary Louise. *Joy and Wonder, Love and Longing.* Chicago: GIA Publications, 2002.

Duck, Ruth. *Dancing in the Universe.* Chicago: GIA Publications, 1992.

Nyberg, Anders. *Freedom Is Coming: Songs of Protest and Praise from South Africa.* Glasgow: Wild Goose Publishing, 1990.

Thomas, Lisa Neufeld, ed. *Voices Found: Women in the Church's Song.* New York: Church Publishing, 2003.

Recordings

Desert Wind. *World Dance.* Desert Wind, 1999.

HARC. *HARC: Inside Chants.* HARC, 2004.

Libana. *Fire Within.* Ladyslipper, 1990.

Monks of Keur Moussa Abbey. *Keur Moussa: Sacred Chants and African Rhythms from Senegal.* Sounds True, 1997.

Mickey Hart, *Planet Drum.* Rykodisc, 1991.

Global Meditation. *Harmony and Interplay Ensembles: A Collection of Spiritual, Ritual, and Meditative Music.* Ellipsis Arts, 1992.

SEVEN

SPEAKING AND LISTENING TO THE HOLY: PRAYER

Holy One, you are very great.

. . . You make the clouds your chariot,

you ride on the wings of the wind,

you make the winds your messengers,

fire and flame your ministers.

—Psalm 104:1, 3–4

THINKING ABOUT SPEAKING AND LISTENING

Prayer is simply conversation. Granted, it is conversation with the Holy One, who is creator and sustainer of all that is, so not just any kind of conversation. But it is best to begin by thinking about the character of ordinary conversations, in their simplicity as well as their complexity, before we turn our thoughts to divine conversation.

The best conversations we can think of are, at heart, occasions of reciprocity. We engage both in speaking and in listening. When we speak, we aim to be as truthful and clear as possible. When we listen, we aim to be as attentive and compassionate as we can. And when both conversation partners aim for both, then true conversation takes place. Such occasions, we know, can be quite rare. They grow best in the soil of radical equality, in a relationship of equals. But when they happen, we have a glimpse of what divine conversation can be.

In terms of content, conversations may either offer something (information, encouragement, or thanks, for example) or request something (help, facts, or advice, for example). These same categories apply to prayer conversation as well. That is, we might offer something to the Holy One in prayer: thanks, praise, gifts. Or we might ask for something from the Holy One in prayer: healing, forgiveness, protection, or simply to be heard. But when we begin to think of conversation in terms of conversation with the Holy One, creator and sustainer of the universe, we begin to wonder, what can the nature of such conversation be? If the best conversations are heart-to-heart, in honest speaking and compassionate listening, how can such a radically equal conversation take place between humans and the Holy? Traditionally this dilemma of difference has been resolved by assigning to God the status of a human ruler or authority of some kind: king, father, or master, and by assuming that if the Holy One has much power, we humans (or other beings) must have less.

But must difference always be symbolized by hierarchical models and zero-sum definitions of power? What if difference is just that: difference in kind, in substance, in any other category we care to name? What if the difference between humans and the Holy One is like the difference between humans and a hawk, for example, or a deer, or a bear, or a whale? Once we ask this question, we recognize that other religious cultures have made precisely that identification, as has our own. God is like an eagle; God is like a mother bear; God is like a tiny seed.

This approach to understanding the One to whom we pray invites another model for prayer, that of encounter. And in encounters between unlike beings, speech is likely not the best means, or at least the only means, of communication. We may still understand this encounter as conversation, but now the meaning of the word conversation must shift. The language must shift, and the temporal context must shift, and the spatial context must shift.

Verbal language, the language of spoken words, is only one form of language. There are many others.

There is the language of gesture, movement, and posture: a language of bodies that we also use among humans and at times in our encounters with nonhuman animals. The shift of body weight on the back of a horse, the movement of hand or eye to a dog or cat—we have some familiarity with this language. Among humans, we use body language extensively, including not only gesture and movement, but also our very expressive facial muscles.

There is also the language of color and light. This is a language widely used by birds, who seek out food sources, at least in part, by color. Hummingbirds famously seek sources of food that are colored red, and they can be enticed to include among the red flowers they feed from your backyard feeder made of red plastic. Humans make use of this language also when we wear bright colors to express (or create) feelings of joy and celebration or subdued and dark colors to express sorrow. All living beings respond to light and darkness and require both in order to live and grow. Humans use light and darkness not only for cycles of work and rest, but also for artistic and dramatic expressions.

Then there is the language of scent. The power of pheromones is found among insects, plants, and mammals, as olfactory communication that can convey alarm, territorial limits, or sexual availability. Insects and nonhuman mammals depend on this means of communication for survival. For humans, much olfactory communication

typically takes place at a level beyond (or below) conscious awareness, but we often employ scents intentionally to affect the environment, to express peace or sensuality or to stimulate appetite.

Conversations, then, can take place in a wide variety of languages, languages in which we as human beings of particular cultural
and linguistic groups may not be fluent or even conversant. How
much more complex, and even alien, is the language in which we
converse with the Holy One?

The history of Christian prayer, especially public prayer, has
made use of all of these languages at some time or another. We have
used words: spoken and amplified and intensified, at times, with
music. We have used sounds: bells, drums, organs, and harps. We
have used gestures: bowing, making signs of the cross, lifting our
hands in praise, clasping our hands in entreaty. We have used color
in priestly vestments and banners and glass and paint. We have used
light, in darkened chapels and rooms full of light, in candles and in
light filtered through colored glass. We have used scent: incense,
candle wax, perfumed oil. And sometimes, when our need to be
heard was intense, we have used them all at once.

And of course, in addition to these, or better, as a complement
to these, we have used silence: silence of our own prayer, silent waiting on the response from the Holy One. And in our waiting, we do
well to remember that we are beings who live short and hasty lives,
compared to the everlasting life of God. Our human interactions
teach us of the power of silence as a means of communication: the
companionable silence of dear friends, the expectant silence that
draws out true conversation, the patient silence in times of pain. We
know that silence is not absence of communication, but yet another
language of communication.

If we use all these languages in order to communicate, not only
with one another but also with the Holy One, is it possible that the
Holy One, in turn, might choose to communicate with us by means
of the same languages? Because we often give priority to verbal communication, and because prayer, Christian prayer, has traditionally
focused on worded prayer, we sometimes assume that the Holy One
will respond in like kind. But we do well to learn to be attentive to
the many languages around us, languages in which the Holy One

may choose to speak to us: in sound, in silence, in breath of air, in song of bird, in scent, in light, and in darkness.

The wisdom discovered through feminist ritual pathways may provide helpful guidelines in thinking about prayer as this rich conversation with the Holy One. The wisdom of our lives teaches us to long for true conversation, to hold fast to what poet Adrienne Rich calls "a dream of a common language." We cannot be content with language of prayer that is banal, superficial, inauthentic, or manipulative. The wisdom of our bodies teaches us to seek communication that employs all our senses and that, in employing them, honors them. This bodied wisdom teaches us to give careful attention to the nonverbal aspects of prayer, lest we incorporate, literally, behaviors of submission and passivity. It teaches us to embody and enact our prayers with joy and fearlessness. The wisdom of our suffering and struggle cautions us to take care that our use of prayer be attentive to the needs of others who also suffer and struggle, to be open to learning from others, to listen attentively and with compassion. This wisdom encourages us to explore means of practicing resistance to suffering (our own as well as that of others) by learning forms of lament, exorcism, and even curses, and by learning practices of blessings for those who resist with courage and grace. The wisdom of our relationships teaches us the values of openness, honesty, patience, and compassion, and shows us the blessings of true conversations of the heart as models for our prayers to the Holy One and as means by which the Holy One may choose to speak to us. Our relational wisdom also teaches us to attend to our connections to the nonhuman world in which we are enmeshed, to listen for their voices, however different from ours, to learn from their lives, to see in them new possibilities for communication with the Holy One.

A SPIRITUAL DISCIPLINE OF SPEAKING AND LISTENING

In addition to the spiritual disciplines for sound suggested in the previous chapter, we can sharpen our ability to attend to the many languages that surround us. Sound is only one of them. Here are some suggestions for practices that can attune us to other languages.

1. *Take a walk in the light.* Moving in a quiet, attentive, and meditative manner through any space can be a means of opening the senses to the multiple languages around us. Focus attention particularly on color and light during a walk, noting both natural and human-made variations and use of both. It is desirable, but not absolutely necessary, to walk outdoors in order to attend to color and light. If an indoor space includes ample natural light, being in an enclosed space can enhance one's attention to the ways in which light and darkness interplay and affect our appropriation of color. Pay particular attention to the effect of light and color on your focus, on your body, on your mind, on your feelings. How do color and light communicate with you?

2. *Take time to attend to scents.* This might be done as part of a regular routine, such as cooking or bathing. Take time to notice and pay attention to the scent of food, of soap, focusing on the ways in which different scents affect your mind and your emotions and how they communicate with you. A walk through a produce aisle or farmer's market offers many opportunities to experience different scents, as does time spent in a garden or other natural spot.

3. *Learn another language.* Learning to speak another language can have the double benefit of introducing one to another way of expressing the world and of offering new insight about one's first language.

4. *Attend to the needs of the world.* The practice of intercessory prayer demands that we learn to focus our attention on the needs of the world in which we live and of which we are a part. Reading the newspapers, attending to cries of the suffering

around the world (including the suffering of the earth and its nonhuman inhabitants as well as human beings), and learning the needs of our local communities are necessary disciplines for a strong intercessory prayer life.

5. *Keep a prayer journal.* Make notes on what needs require intercession and action. Note times and places that you have experienced the presence of the Holy One. Be open to the Holy One in unexpected places and speaking through unfamiliar voices or in untraditional languages.

The spiritual disciplines suggested in "Bodies" (chapter 5), "Sound" (chapter 6), and "Seasons" (chapter 9) can also be helpful in developing intentional practices to strengthen one's ability to pray using all one's senses for listening to and speaking with the Holy One.

PATTERNS FOR SPEAKING AND LISTENING: Prayer

Patterns for Spoken Prayer: Thanksgiving

A classic and very simple ancient prayer form, common to Judaism and Christianity, is the *berakah/hodayah* form. Its name derives from its first word in Hebrew, either "blessed" (*berakah*) or "thanks" (*hodayah*). Its structure follows an easily remembered pattern:

1. Blessing or thanksgiving
   Blessed are you or
   Thanks be to you

2. Naming
   Holy One

3. Deed
   You bring forth food from the earth

The prayer may end here, with a simple repetition of the opening blessing or declaration of thanks. Or it may be expanded with the addition of a more detailed recalling of the works of the Holy One that leads into a request and a promise.

4. Remembrance
   You feed all who call upon you; while we wandered in the wilderness, you fed us with manna from heaven, etc.

5. Request
   Feed us now, we beg you.

6. Promise
   We will praise your graciousness forever and ever.

This is a pattern that is highly flexible and adaptable to almost any circumstance that demands a prayer of praise or thanksgiving. In its briefest form, this is a pattern that need not include a request or petition of any kind. It serves well as a prayer practice focused on cultivating a spirit of gratitude. When the additional remembrance and request are added, it has the benefit of placing our requests in the larger context of God's gifts to us, giving us hopeful shape to our cries for help.

This prayer form is the foundation of the Christian eucharistic prayer, the Great Thanksgiving, and the prototypical Christian expression of thanks. Examples of eucharistic prayers are found in chapter 11, "Meals."

Patterns for Spoken Prayer: Petition and Intercession

As those baptized into the community of equals, as residents in Wisdom's house, we have the responsibility and the power to intercede on behalf of the world before the Holy One. This responsibility works itself out in many ways, including political and social action, works of love and mercy, and our efforts to bring our daily lives into harmony with Wisdom's work for the well-being of all creatures of earth. One of the ways that we can do this, and also ground our active work on behalf of the world, is to pray with intention for the world. In traditional terms, this is called intercessory prayer, which has long been considered a basic responsibility of the baptized. Although classical prayer has made a distinction between prayers of petition, in which one asks for something for oneself, and prayers of intercession, in which one asks for something for others, in the community of equals such distinctions fade. The aim of our prayer is to leap such boundaries and to see the world as whole and ourselves as part of the whole. And while we must ask the Holy One for our own needs—and why not?—we also come to see those personal, individual, or local needs as part of much larger patterns of needs and longing for wholeness.

Prayer of intercession may follow a pattern that takes a spiral form, beginning either with the outer circle of the universe and the earth, and moving into our local and personal needs, or beginning locally and moving outward to embrace the whole world. A typical pattern would look like this:

1. Opening prayer, inviting community intercessions

2. For the earth, its healing and well-being

3. For the nations, for peace and understanding among them

4. For our nation, for wise and just leaders

5. For our city, town, community

6. For this church in her house, for wisdom and courage

7. For those who suffer

8. For those who have died

9. For our own needs

10. Closing prayer

The order of intercessions 2–9 may be reversed if it seems desirable to begin at the personal local level and work outward to the earth. These are very broad categories and might be broken into more specific petitions and requests as seems appropriate and as there is awareness of needs.

Patterns for Spoken Prayer: Lament

We do not always come before the Holy One with mouths full of praise or hearts full of thanksgiving or even hope. When thanksgiving and praise are not appropriate, when cries for deliverance have already been made, in times of great distress and suffering, prayers of lament are called for. Although somewhat rare in the broader tradition of Christian prayer, the book of Psalms is full of prayers of lament, complaints against God for undeserved suffering, expressions of sorrow for irredeemable loss, demands that God hear our complaints and judge evildoers and bring them to justice. These laments require very little adaptation to express contemporary laments. They include these elements:

1. A demand or request for help

2. A lament for what has already been suffered or lost

3. A declaration (based on past experience) of trust

4. A specific petition (often a call to God to bear witness to suffering and loss)

5. A promise of praise (often provisional, dependent on God's response to the petition)

Biblical lament psalms fall into two categories: individual and corporate or communal. Individual psalms of lament include these:

3, 4, 5, 7, 9, 10, 13, 14, 17, 22, 25, 26, 27, 28, 31, 35, 36, 39, 41, 42, 43, 52, 53, 54, 55, 56, 57, 59, 61, 63, 64, 69, 70, 71, 77, 86, 88, 109, 120, 139, 140, 141, and 142. Communal laments include these: 12, 44, 58, 60, 74, 79, 80, 83, 85, 90, 94, 123, 126, 129, and 137. When you read through these psalms, especially the communal laments, you might be shocked that some of them call for God to punish one's enemies harshly and that some of them accuse God of sleeping and failing to hear or to act. We do not often hear these psalms or these portions of psalms in worship. But if we claim the responsibility to intercede for the world before the Holy One, such challenging prayers need to be part of our vocabulary. By placing judgment and punishment in God's hands, we take these acts out of our human hands. By challenging God to act in the face of suffering, we acknowledge that the world is not yet whole and healed, and we affirm our partnership with the Holy One in bringing about this healing.

Patterns for Nonverbal Prayer

Praying with all our senses can deepen and strengthen our prayer as individuals and as communities, and it can help us learn to be more attentive to the myriad ways that the Holy One may choose to communicate with us. Here are some suggestions for nonverbal prayer that may serve as prayers in and of themselves or as part of spoken prayer.

Burning incense

The burning of something scented in order to produce smoke and a pleasing smell is found in many religions, where it is connected not only with prayer but also with purification. The incense itself may be understood as both a means of prayer and as an expression of our connection with the earth. Incense materials may include fragrant tree sap (myrrh, for example), wood permeated with fragrant oils or essences, aromatic herbs or wood, and the like. It is possible to purchase prepared incense, but it is also possible to make one's own by bundling together herbs such as sage, rosemary, or whatever herbs might be grown locally. The smoke from the incense rises, signifying our prayers rising to heaven.

Scented oil or water

Another means of using scent as a form of prayer is in the use of scented oil or water. Here the scent is part of the use of oil for anointing or water for washing, as enacted prayers or as part of spoken prayers. The use of scented oil is often part of baptismal and healing rites (see chapter 10, "Entering into Community," and chapter 12, "Healing," for further examples). But either oil or water can also be part of prayers apart from these rites. Try, for example, using a small basin of warm water, with a small amount of aromatic oil added, for a hand-washing ritual as a morning or evening personal prayer.

Gestures with the hands

Prayer gestures using the hands are also ancient and found in many religions. Traditional gestures include lifting the hands at shoulder height, folding the hands on the breast, clasping the hands together, and making a small cross gesture with the finger or thumb on parts of the body being blessed. Any of these gestures is a prayer in itself, simple, complete, and expressive. Try one of these before or after a meal. Prayers of lament call for more aggressive hand gestures, including shaking fists or clenching fists.

Gestures with the whole body

Many traditional prayer movements imply submission: bowing the head to expose the neck, bowing at the waist or kneeling to lower one's height before a superior, prostrating oneself on the floor to signify abasement. We can seek alternatives to these submissive gestures by employing postures of confidence, hope, and challenge: standing with eyes lifted up, dancing, walking to signify movement in the Spirit, joining hands as a mark of solidarity and community, and so on. Prayers of lament call for bodily expressions of mourning or accusation, including weeping and wordless cries. Additional examples for whole body prayer can be found in chapter 5, "Bodies."

Walking

Walking also can serve as prayer itself, if undertaken with attentiveness and reflection, and a meditative walk by an individual or a community is a powerful prayer. But walking, either meditatively or in procession, is also an ancient element of spoken prayers. Processional prayer, in which an individual or community moves prayerfully from one "station" to another for prayer, singing while moving, not only employs two modes of prayer (spoken/sung word and movement), but also marks out sacred space as well. Such prayer processions invite focus on the activities associated with that space, whether the prayer stations are urban locations of political and social power or lack of power, or natural places of beauty or destruction. By bringing together prayer of words with prayer of movement and space, intense attention is focused on the life of that place, and Holy Wisdom is invoked.

Many people find walking a labyrinth to be a valuable and powerful means of prayer with the body, where the path of concentric, interconnected circles leading to the center can move one from an outward orientation to an inward, reflective perspective, and then back out. Labyrinths can be found in many churches, both indoors, set into the floor, and outdoors, in a garden or other open space. A finger labyrinth—a small handheld pattern of a labyrinth—makes this physical prayer available when walking a labyrinth is not possible or practical.

PRAYERS FOR SPEAKING AND LISTENING

A PRAYER FOR THE PRESENCE OF THE HOLY ONE

Holy One,
you speak, and worlds come into existence;
you act, and the waters leap and the earth dances.
Show yourself to us
in word and in silence,
in act and in gesture,
in the things of creation
and in the things we have made;
so that all our words and silences,
all our gestures and deeds,
reveal your beauty and grace
to all the world.
Blessed are you, Holy One,
and blessed is your Wisdom,
now and forever.

A PRAYER OF THANKSGIVING FOR UNDERSTANDING

God of wisdom and understanding:
you give us minds to think
and hearts to love;
may all of our thinking and loving
be to your greater glory
and to the glory of your Wisdom,
Jesus Christ,
who lives and reigns with you and the Holy Spirit,
one God,
now and forever.

A LITANY OF INTERCESSION

(This litany may be prayed as part of a Sunday gathering, either at the beginning of the service or following the service of the Word. When it precedes the service of Holy Communion, it may be prayed as the community processes to gather around the table.)

With heart, mind, and body we pray to the Holy One, saying (singing), "Hear us, we pray."

For the healing of the earth: for clear water, clean air, for life in all its variety, we pray to the Holy One.

Hear us, we pray.

For the healing of the nations: for peace, justice, understanding, for life in all its variety, we pray to the Holy One.

Hear us, we pray.

For the healing of the Church: for wisdom, welcome, love, courage, for faith in all its variety, we pray to the Holy One.

Hear us, we pray.

For those who suffer, in our midst and in our world: for relief, justice, rest, and renewal, we pray to the Holy One.

Hear us, we pray.

For the needs of this community, named and held silently in our hearts:

(Here members of the community may call out names of those in need.)

Hear us, we pray.

For those who have died: peace, rest, and light, we pray to the Holy One.

Hear us, we pray.

In the communion of all the holy ones who have gone before us, let us commend ourselves, and one another, and the whole world to the Wisdom of God, Jesus Christ.

To you, Holy Wisdom.

A Great Litany for Penitential Days

(This litany, based on the Great Litany in the Book of Common Prayer, is intended for use during seasons or occasions of self-reflection and repentance or during a time of troubles. It can be prayed in a procession, and burning of incense may accompany the prayer, combining prayer in words, prayer in movement, and prayer in scent.)

Holy One, Creator of all that is,

have mercy on us.

Holy Wisdom, Jesus Christ,

have mercy on us.

Holy Spirit, breath of life,

have mercy on us.

Forget our failures and our sins. Remember your love for your world. Spare us and spare your world, by your mercy.

Spare us, Holy One.

From all oppression, from all injustice, from all who seek to do us harm,

Holy One, deliver us.

From all willful ignorance, from hatred, fear, insult, and suspicion,

Holy One, deliver us.

From all harmful doctrine, from hurtful teachings and hateful preaching,

Holy One, deliver us.

From disaster, disease, and injury to life and limb; from attack, invasion, rape and battering,

Holy One, deliver us.

By the mystery of the stars and of the cells, by the wonder of the heavens and the molecules,

Holy One, deliver us.

By the turn of the sunflower and the power of the seed, by
the opening of the bloom and the setting of the fruit, by
the roots in the earth and the leaves in the sun,

Holy One, deliver us.

By the song of the swallow and the cry of the wolf, by the
hum of the whale and the call of the wild goose,

Holy One, deliver us.

By the laugh of the child and the kiss of the lover, by the
touch of the parent and the handclasp of the friend, by
the shared struggle of the companion,

Holy One, deliver us.

In our joys and in our griefs, in all our troubles and in all our
triumphs, in our life and in our death and in our hope
and in our fear,

Holy One, deliver us.

We implore you to hear us, Holy One, and to guide and help
your people of wisdom in all the earth.

Holy One, deliver us.

Fill the leaders of all religious communities with your
wisdom and inspire them to teach it and live it out.

Hear us, Holy One.

Bless the people of all religious communities with wise and
understanding hearts.

Hear us, Holy One.

Show all people your deep wisdom and guide them to live
together in harmony and peace.

Hear us, Holy One.

Bring all who turn away from your Wisdom and reject your
peace into companionship with you.

Hear us, Holy One.

Guide the leaders of this nation, that they may find your wisdom and seek to do justice, love mercy, and walk in your ways.

Hear us, Holy One.

May the leaders of all nations and peoples bring an end to war and enmity, and choose peace and justice.

Hear us, Holy One.

May all prisoners and captives be released, all homeless and hungry be sheltered and fed, all who are lost and oppressed find hope and freedom.

Hear us, Holy One.

May the earth give its bounty generously, and may all farmers, ranchers, growers, and preparers of our food work in harmony with your good earth.

Hear us, Holy One.

May all who labor do so with integrity, wisdom, and good will, and for the common good.

Hear us, Holy One.

May all who travel, work, or serve in harm's way be kept in safety.

Hear us, Holy One.

May all women in childbirth, all infants and young children, those who are at risk and those who suffer, be protected and preserved in safety.

Hear us, Holy One.

May those who are alone, those who are isolated, those who suffer in silence, those who are abandoned, those who are rejected, find comfort and companionship.

Hear us, Holy One.

Have mercy on all humankind, on all that run on four feet, on all that swim, on all that fly, on all that live below the earth, on all that move upon the earth.

Hear us, Holy One.

Forgive our negligence, our forgetfulness, our failure to care for our neighbors and our earth; give us true repentance; fill us with your strong Spirit to bring about the peace and justice for which we pray.

Hear us, Holy One.

Forgive our enemies, persecutors, and attackers, and turn their hearts to your peace and justice.

Hear us, Holy One.

Give our beloved dead rest and peace in your light.

Hear us, Holy One.

When we come to our rest at the end, grant us your peace and light.

Hear us, Holy One.

Holy Wisdom, Jesus Christ, we implore you to hear us.

Holy Wisdom, Jesus Christ, we implore you to hear us.

Lamb of God, that takes on the suffering of the world,

Have mercy on us,

Lamb of God, that takes on the suffering of the world,

Have mercy on us,

Lamb of God, that takes on the suffering of the world,

Grant us your peace.

Oh Christ, hear us.

Oh Christ, hear us.

Holy One, have mercy on us.
Wisdom, have mercy on us.
Holy One, have mercy on us.
Holy One, show us your mercy,

as we put our trust in you.

Holy One:
you have promised to hear the prayers
of those who ask in the name of your Wisdom, Jesus Christ.
We implore you to hear us now.
We implore you to grant our requests
and to keep us always in your care;
through Jesus Christ,
our companion and your Wisdom.

RESOURCES FOR SPEAKING AND LISTENING: PRAYER

Anderson, Bernhard W. *Out of the Depths: The Psalms Speak for Us Today*. Philadelphia: Westminster Press, 1983.

Meyers, Ruth A., and Phoebe Pettingell, eds. *Gleanings: Essays on Expansive Language with Prayers for Various Occasions*. New York: Church Publishing, 2001.

Morley, Janet. *All Desires Known: Inclusive Prayers for Worship and Meditation*. Expanded ed. Harrisburg, Pa.: Morehouse Publishing, 1988, 1992.

A New Zealand Prayer Book. He Karakia Mihinare O Aotearoa. New York: HarperCollins, 1993.

Procter-Smith, Marjorie. *Praying With Our Eyes Open: Engendering Feminist Liturgical Prayer*. Nashville: Abingdon Press, 1995.

Winter, Miriam Therese. *WomanPrayer, WomanSong: Resources for Ritual*. New York: Meyer Stone/Crossroad, 1987.

EIGHT

SPEAKING AND LISTENING TO THE HOLY: SCRIPTURE

Take my instruction instead of silver,

And knowledge rather than choice gold;

For Wisdom is better than jewels,

And all that you desire cannot compare with her.

—Proverbs 8:10–11

THINKING ABOUT SCRIPTURE

The Bible as Mixed Blessing

The Christian tradition has privileged the Bible over all other sacred writings, making it the foundation stone of Christian life and worship. For many of us, our first encounter with the promise of freedom and well-being was mediated by a scripture text: "For freedom Christ has set us free. Stand firm, therefore, and do not submit again to a yoke of slavery." "There is no longer Jew or Greek, there is no longer slave or free, there is no longer male or female; for all of you are one in Christ Jesus." "Blessed is she who believed that there would be a fulfillment of what was spoken to her by the Lord." "Mary Magdalene went and announced to the disciples: 'I have seen the Lord.'" For some of us, this emancipatory Word did not come until we first heard the Bible read in an inclusive translation, so that the texts that formerly appeared to address others now, stunningly, spoke directly to us. The Bible can come to us as emancipatory Word, as a revelatory encounter with the One who frees us, with Wisdom's teaching, with the love of Jesus, Mary's child.

But we also have experienced the harmful effects of scripture: hateful proscriptions against homosexuality, restrictions against women's freedom, support for slavery systems, advocacy of submission in varied forms. Even texts that may seem harmless to one group may have been used against another. What's more, the almost unremitting male dominance of the narratives, the voices, the perspectives, and the ideas found in scripture intensifies our alienation from the texts and even from the whole Bible. Because we live within such a long tradition in which these male-centered texts have been interpreted in ways that further support male dominance, because we have experienced the damage that can be done by a reading of the text that silences and vilifies and marginalizes so many of us, we understandably want to reject the Bible as a whole. Because we have often been told by those who insist on the infallibility of the written texts, of their whole and divinely inspired origins, that we must accept and believe all of it, we are sometimes inclined to accept the apparent alternative: none of it.

The church in her house, of course, is an image that draws on biblical stories: the depiction of God, or of an aspect of God, as a woman named Wisdom, or Sophia. It also draws on often ignored or hidden stories in the New Testament of early house-churches that met in the homes of women and that had women as leaders. How, then, do we adjudicate between these positions: shall we accept the canonical Christian scriptures as Word of God, or shall we reject them?

We first acknowledge our ambivalence about the Bible, that at times it seems life-giving and at other times dangerously harmful. We also acknowledge the presence of the voices of the marginalized: of women, of the poor, of children, of slaves, of homosexual persons, of persons with disabilities, as being hidden within the texts. Women, children, slaves, the poor, and, no doubt, homosexual persons all were among those who first heard and responded to the message of Jesus, were among those who knew the tradition of Wisdom, were among those who influenced and perhaps even wrote some of the texts that are now part of the Bible. That these same stories, these same texts, have misrepresented, maligned, or marginalized these same people should not unduly surprise us, as this still happens. Who has not had the experience of having our own stories turned against us?

The church in her house, therefore, seeks to free these hidden voices, to move these marginalized persons to the center, to claim Wisdom's treasure of knowledge and welcome. What does Wisdom teach us about scripture, about sacred texts? What have we learned already through the wisdom of our bodies, our experiences, our struggles, and our relationships?

Our experiences of oppression and our own practical religious experiences enable us to approach sacred texts with an eye toward seeing those voices that have been oppressed and silenced, and we can recognize the construction of practical religious experience among those who have been marginalized. So, for example, we might read the story in Jeremiah of the women of Israel making cakes to offer to the "Queen of Heaven" as an example of this practical religious experience, a way of keeping one's people and children safe (see Jer.7:18, 44:15–19). So we might notice that the daughters of Philip are described as prophets in Acts 21:9, but neither are they named nor is any word of prophecy attributed to them, but instead to "a [male] prophet named Agabus." Our experience of oppression and silencing gives us the ability to read sacred texts with a degree of suspicion: What has been left out? What has been distorted in the telling? Whose stories are absent, whose voices silent? This suspicion also enables us to challenge the authority of written words, since we know how easily they may be twisted. The texts do not govern us: we choose the texts and stories that give life and reject the texts that are toxic. Although we claim the whole Bible as our story, it is a story that is distorted, misused, a story of pain and harm as well as a story of life and well-being.

The wisdom of our bodies helps us to understand the stories of healing in the Christian scriptures as stories of hope for wholeness and well-being. This wisdom also grants us insight into the stories of violence. Alas, the rape of Tamar by her brother, the murder of the Levite's concubine as a means to protect men from violence, the betrayal of Jephtha's daughter by her own father, the rape and abduction of women in time of war and as a normal part of conquest: all of these stories are not only ancient tales but stories happening now. We recognize them, in our bodies. And we also recognize the healing stories: the impoverished widow whose child is brought back to life by the prophet Elijah, the woman who is empowered by Jesus to stand up straight and praise the Holy One, the distraught parents who rejoice when Jesus restores their young daughter to life. We know these stories through our longing for them in our bodies.

The wisdom of our relationships with one another, and with the natural world of which we are a part, also leads us to see sacred writings as a means to expand that relationship to encompass those we don't know, or those who are long dead, or those whose lives and stories are radically different from our own. Sacred scriptures can open us to experiences that we cannot know in our bodies, stories we can understand only through the exercise of empathy and compassion.

Emancipating the Bible

We are challenged to recognize in the Bible the story, however partial and distorted, of our people, and the foundational text of our Christian faith. We are also challenged to handle it with caution, since we know that it has been and continues to be dangerous to women, children, gay and lesbian people, persons with disabilities, the poor, and many others. We can claim it as our own story only if we are willing to do the difficult work of emancipating the Bible from its kyriarchal context, seeking the hidden and silenced stories and placing them at the center of the community. The first step in this emancipatory process is to recognize that the Word of God is not limited to written words on a page. The Word of God is active, powerful, and life-giving, and it is present in the midst of the community, when that community is willing to open itself to that Word. We should remind ourselves that in the Gospel of John Jesus is identified as the Word, the Word made flesh, so that we can know the Word of God through Jesus, who is risen and present in the midst of us. Recognizing the Word in our midst, in the community, in one another, in our selves, is the first step in emancipating the Bible. The Bible is only a written record, by many people, from their limited perspectives. By claiming the presence of the living Word in the community and seeking its liberating power we can free the written Word from the page.

We do this, first of all, when we speak the texts aloud, giving the words flesh and sound. The one who reads the sacred text in some sense becomes that text, incarnates that text, in the unique context and within the unique community where the reading takes place. The one who reads the text also restores the text to its original context, since most of the writings of the Bible were first oral accounts, passed along by word of mouth; even letters were written to be read aloud. And in giving voice to the texts, we free them from the page and open them to interact with us, and us with them, as living Word.

We also free the Word when we preach, discuss, or interpret the text in community. Within feminist emancipatory communities, there can be no authoritative single voice from the pulpit, offering the only correct reading of the text. Rather, the Word is released into the community by its being embodied and made present by the reader, and then taken up by the community members who not only hear the Word, but also become the Word themselves as they converse with the text. Feminist emancipatory preaching is ultimately a conversation. The form that this conversation takes will depend on the needs and decisions of the community as to the best way to make the Word present in its midst.

Other Wise Words

When we recognize the incomplete and contingent character of the Christian scriptures, we open up the possibility that Wisdom may teach us through other written texts as well. We can seek Wisdom through other ancient Christian writings that were not accepted into the modern Christian canon, open to the Word as it may make itself known to us: the Gospel of Mary, the Acts of Paul and Thecla, the Gospel of Thomas, the Shepherd of Hermas—all these and more early Christian writings show us a broader range of ideas and stories than the ones included in the traditional scriptures. Here, Mary Magdalene argues with Peter over authority in the church; Thecla baptizes herself and names herself missionary; the risen Jesus speaks secret words; a visionary encounters a powerful and wise female guide and teacher.

We also recognize the teaching of Wisdom through nonbiblical spiritual writings. The writings of women mystics and spiritual leaders such as Teresa of Avila, Mechtilde of Magdeburg, Hildegard of Bingen, Julian of Norwich, Sister Jarena Lee, Margaret Fell Fox, along with accounts of the lives of Mother Ann Lee, Sojourner Truth, and Lucretia Mott demonstrate the ongoing work of Wisdom.

And we are open to finding the teachings of Wisdom in contemporary writings, such as the works of Alice Walker, Barbara Kingsolver, Adrienne Rich, Anne Cameron, Esther Broner, and many others. Feminist emancipatory communities will develop their own canon of supplementary holy writings in which they have found the words of Wisdom through disciplined feminist Bible study and intentional reading practices.

A SPIRITUAL DISCIPLINE OF READING AND HEARING SCRIPTURE

A spiritual discipline of embodying the Word requires prayerful preparation, intelligent study, and respectful listening to one another. It also requires choosing which texts we will allow to be spoken and made present in our communities and which texts will not be given the status of holy Word.

A Spiritual Discipline of Emancipatory Discernment

Emancipatory discernment, as outlined in chapter 1, "Pathways and Signposts," can be useful in the process of choosing texts to be granted sacred status. Especially critical to this process in choosing scripture is the employment of feminist emancipatory criteria: Who benefits from choosing this text? Who suffers? Where are the women? The children? Others who have been marginalized and silenced? Are they present? Are their voices heard? What about the voiceless: those who are far away, those who are absent, the members of the community of the earth and the environment? Who speaks for them?

Because we know how much power has been granted to these texts of the Bible, we will be both patient and honest with those who struggle to refuse any biblical texts. Because we have all been harmed at some time or another by traditional biblical texts or their interpretation, we will be both honest and patient with those who struggle to accept any biblical texts. Using the feminist ritual pathways and Christian signposts described in chapter 1 can aid in working through this process, applying these steps to a biblical text or book. The common reading of feminist emancipatory biblical studies resources (some are listed at the end of this chapter) and the establishment of an ongoing scripture study class can also provide depth of understanding and common discussion of the issues at stake.

A Spiritual Discipline of Feminist Emancipatory Bible Study

Feminist emancipatory Bible study is part unlearning what we have been told about the Bible and part opening ourselves up to new interpretations and approaches. Wisdom offers instruction and insight. But our own mental efforts are required too. The church in her house can provide opportunities for emancipatory Bible study in the form of study groups, classes, retreats, and visiting lecturers and teachers.

A Spiritual Discipline of Emancipatory *Lectio Divina*

Traditional practices of *lectio divina*, an ancient Christian discipline of reading and praying canonical scripture, presuppose the authority of the Christian canon. Since feminist emancipatory communities question this authority and claim the authority to affirm or reject portions of the canon, the traditional practice requires adaptation. In place of submission to the authority of the text, we claim our own authority to recognize texts that are harmful and texts that are life-giving. In place of uncritical reading, we exercise our critical interpretive skills. But from the ancient tradition we claim the savoring of a powerful text and the process of allowing prayer to grow organically out of our direct encounter with the Wisdom found in the Word.

Personal emancipatory lectio divina

- Choose a brief text. It may be from canonical scripture, extra-canonical scripture, spiritual writings, or contemporary writings.

- Read it aloud to yourself, slowly.

- Think about the text; write down any questions or puzzles that come to you.

- Pray for wisdom and insight.

Communal emancipatory lectio divina

- In a small group, members may take turns choosing the brief text.

- One person reads the text aloud, slowly, while the others listen prayerfully.

- Each person thinks about the text and writes down any questions that come to mind.

- The reader reads the text again.

- Each person reflects silently on their own questions.

- The reader reads the text again.

- Each one prays silently for wisdom.

- If desired, group members may share their questions or insights about the text.

- The reader or some other member of the group closes the session with a prayer for wisdom.

A Spiritual Discipline of Embodying the Word

The one who reads the Word in community has the opportunity to give flesh and voice to the Wisdom of the Word. Since this is a responsibility that is shared by all members of the community, all should be engaged in a discipline of preparing to read. Here are a few suggestions for such preparation:

Read aloud

We now live in a primarily visual rather than oral culture. The art of reading aloud is a lost art. One may recover this practice by reading aloud to oneself, to family members, or to friends. The literature being read is less important that the act of reading with care, intelligence, and intentionality.

Read intentionally

Because words are powerful, one should exercise intentionality about what one reads for pleasure. Because our imaginations have been colonized by kyriarchal thinking and teaching, one should choose reading material that expands our imaginations and challenges the structures of kyriarchal domination. Writings by women, by writers not of the dominant race or ethnicity or nationality, by writers who are disabled or poor or otherwise marginalized, by writers from other cultures than the dominant culture—these writings can help us open our imaginations to other worlds and can often provide a window into better understanding of our own lives.

Form groups to choose readings for worship and for other gatherings

An egalitarian process for selecting texts for community readings can be constructed by soliciting recommendations from members of the community for readings or for adapting existing lectionary systems. Learn to "read between the lines" of the kyriarchal texts; develop practices of storytelling, song and dance, drama, visual art, and poetry to make present those who have been hidden.

Provide training for those who will read texts aloud in worship gatherings

Opportunities for readers to rehearse their readings, to receive helpful feedback from others, and to experiment with new methods of presenting scripture can enliven the community's encounter with the Word and strengthen the community's sense of responsibility for embodying the Word.

Experiment with presenting the Word in a variety of media

Reading a text aloud has its own power, when it is done well. But some texts may call for the use of additional media, such as changes in light, the use of drums, rhythm instruments, sound effects, different voices, or drama. While this may not be realistic or even desirable on a regular basis, for special events, seasons, or certain texts such enrichment of the text can increase participation and deepen the experience of the text. In order to prevent this from becoming a self-referential performance, steps would need to be taken in the planning to engage the whole community in embodying the text.

PATTERNS OF READING AND HEARING SCRIPTURE:

A Feminist Emancipatory Lectionary

Any system of reading holy texts in gatherings for worship, or even for personal devotion, is a lectionary. Whether you follow an officially constructed set of readings published by a denominational office, use a system devised by an individual, create your own system, or simply let the Bible fall open to a text, you are using a lectionary. The question is not whether to use a lectionary, but what lectionary system to use.

All modern denominational lectionary systems are based on androcentric, or male-centered, models. That is, because they do not include all canonical biblical texts, they must be selective; and the principle of selection is based on including the main stories and central actors of the biblical story. And these major actors are men; these central stories, for the most part, focus on the actions and words of men. Since the Bible as a whole is androcentric, with women falling into the margins and side stories, or, when they are actors, rarely given words to speak, lectionary systems built on this model tend to be even more androcentric than the Bible itself.

Most lectionary systems also assign three or four readings from different sections of the Bible to a given Sunday or feast day. Normally, this means one reading from the Hebrew scriptures, one reading from the New Testament Epistles, and one reading from the Synoptic Gospels, with a Psalm that may serve as a reading or as a congregational song. In selecting these three or four readings, the committees that compiled the lectionaries aim for a common theme or overlapping narrative, or they allow the readings to comment on one another, sometimes for each Sunday, sometimes over a series of many weeks. But this "conversation" between and among the readings serves as its own interpretation. And this interpretation may harmonize or minimize disagreements within the texts, or offer an interpretation that might be different if one were to read the text in its original context.

Therefore, a feminist emancipatory community must bring its interpretive suspicions to bear not only on the biblical text itself, but also on all systems of reading of scripture that are selective and therefore interpretive themselves. Here are some basic principles to keep in mind when constructing a feminist emancipatory lectionary system:

1. Remember that the biblical canon is male-centered in language and imagery and kyriarchal in its context. Where it assumes the subordination of women to men, defends the practice of human slavery, or asserts the unquestioning obedience of children or servants, it works against the life-giving Wisdom of the Word.

2. The hostility of certain texts toward women, children, slaves, and servants should not be minimized or softened, as we continue to live with the consequences of such teachings.

3. The human cost of hostile texts must be recognized, lamented, and repented of in worship, both in the ancient stories themselves and in the use of those stories in the present day.

4. Biblical texts that mute or silence the voices of women and other oppressed groups must be amplified by means of imaginative interpretation in song, dance, prayer, drama, poetry, conversation, and proclamation.

5. The silencing and erasure of women and others from the biblical canon is an ideological move in the interests of kyriarchy, and therefore we acknowledge that the Bible as we have it is distorted and incomplete. We can expand the canon to include other voices of Wisdom as we discover them.

There are many ways that these principles may be put into practice, and each community will want to take responsibility for devising their own best means of giving Wisdom voice. Here are three suggested patterns for constructing a feminist emancipatory lectionary system.

Missing voices

Texts that lack, distort, or obscure the voices of women and other marginalized persons are moved from the margins of the text to the center. In some cases, these voices are present in the text but have been marginalized by androcentric lectionary systems. The daughters of Zelophehad, who claim their father's inheritance, are present in the book of Numbers, remarkably, by name: Mahlah, Noah, Hoglah, Micah, and Tirzah. They pressed their case to Moses before the whole people of Israel, and the Holy One took their side, setting a precedent that daughters may inherit from their father (Num. 27:1–11). This story, found in no modern lectionaries, can stand on its own. But most stories will require the exercise of imagination, not only in recovering the missing voices, but in giving them voice at last, or by calling attention to the silence of the texts.

For example, the daughters of Philip, who are said to be prophets, are given no prophetic words. What would they have said to the church of their time? What would they say to us? Or for another example, the women disciples of Jesus have no call stories to compare with those of the major male disciples. The stories of Peter and Andrew being called from their fishing, the calling of Matthew from collecting taxes for the Romans—these stories are so well known they do not require retelling. But where are the stories of the call of the women disciples? The gospels are silent, but the stories of the male disciples are so dramatic and familiar that we hardly notice this silence. A feminist emancipatory lectionary system would draw attention to this silence in the text or let imagination fill that silence. Another significant textual silence is found in the story of the woman who anoints Jesus' head with fragrant oil, a priestly and prophetic liturgical act. Jesus is recorded as promising that wherever the gospel is proclaimed, her act will be told "in memory of her" (Matt. 26:6–13; Mark 14:3–9). But already when the gospels were written down, her name had been omitted, and the text appears only rarely in modern lectionary systems. A feminist emancipatory lectionary system would lament and correct this betrayal.

Conflicting voices

The Bible is full of self-contradicting texts. But in most lectionary systems, this fact is obscured by the harmonizing tendencies of text selection. Yet only by hearing the disagreements within the Bible, the conflicts reflected in or lying behind biblical texts, can we recognize the complexity of the story we have received and begin to give room for the conflicts and challenges not only in the written word, but in the embodied Word as well. Disagreement is normal, different perspectives abound, and dissent against a single authoritative voice is part of our story. Making room for dissent is an important part of a vital emancipatory community. Resistance against oppression can be found even within or behind oppressive texts. Paul's restrictions against women speaking and teaching is the clearest evidence we could want that such practices were taking place. What if we were to juxtapose, for example, Paul's admonition not to submit to a yoke of slavery (Gal. 5:1) with the instruction in Ephesians 5:22 that wives should submit to their husbands?

Alternative voices

Christian canonical texts can also be contrasted with or paired with noncanonical texts. The Gospel of Mary includes several sections in which Mary Magdalene speaks. These could be read on their own or in combination with canonical Gospel texts about Mary Magdalene or with texts instructing women to keep silent. Contemporary writings can provide poetic or literary readings that can stand on their own as Words of Wisdom or in companionable reading with canonical scripture texts. Making room in our communal readings can model ways of making room for dissenting, silenced, and alternative voices in our midst and in our world.

⊠ PRAYERS FOR READING AND HEARING SCRIPTURE ⊠

A Prayer for Illumination, Addressed to Holy Wisdom

Radiant and unfading Wisdom,
you are intelligent,
holy,
unique,
manifold;
you are more mobile than any motion;
you are a breath of the power of God,
a pure emanation of the Glory of the Holy One.
Enter into our souls;
make us friends of God, and prophets;
teach us, and we shall gain insight;
train us, and we shall learn understanding.
(*from Wisdom of Solomon 6:12, 7:22–27*)

A Prayer for Illumination

Holy One,
open our lips,
open our minds,
show us your Word
in our midst.
We ask in the power of the Spirit
and the name of your Wisdom,
Jesus Christ.

READINGS FOR "CALL STORIES"

Hear how Jesus called Peter and Andrew to be his disciples:
Matthew 4:18–20.

Hear how Jesus called Mary of Magdala to be his disciple:

(*silence*).

Hear how Jesus called James and John to be his disciples:
Matthew 4:21–22.

Hear how Jesus called Mary the mother of James and Joseph
   to be his disciple:

(*silence*).

Hear how Jesus called Matthew to be his disciple:
Matthew 9:9–10.

Hear how Jesus called Salome, and Joanna, and Susannah,
   and many others to be his disciples:

(*silence*).

RESOURCES FOR READING AND HEARING SCRIPTURE

Bowe, Barbara, Kathleen Hughes, Sharon Karam, and Carolyn Osiek. *Silent Voices, Sacred Lives: Women's Readings for the Liturgical Year.* New York: Paulist Press, 1992.

Dube, Musa. *Postcolonial Feminist Interpretation of the Bible.* St. Louis, Mo.: Chalice Press, 2000.

Henderson, J. Frank. *Remembering the Women: Women's Stories from Scripture for Sundays and Festivals.* Chicago: Liturgy Training Publications, 1999.

Lees, Janet. *Word of Mouth: Using the Remembered Bible for Building Community.* Glasgow: Wild Goose Publications, 2006.

Schüssler Fiorenza, Elisabeth. *Wisdom Ways: Introducing Feminist Biblical Interpretation.* Maryknoll, N.Y.: Orbis Books, 2001.

Schüssler Fiorenza, Elisabeth, ed. *Searching the Scriptures: A Feminist Introduction.* New York: Crossroad, 1993.

_____. *Searching the Scriptures: A Feminist Commentary.* New York: Crossroad, 1994.

Sugirtharajah, R. S., ed. *Voices from the Margin: Interpreting the Bible in the Third World.* Maryknoll, N.Y.: Orbis Books, 2006.

Winter, Miriam Therese. *The Chronicles of Noah and her Sisters: Genesis and Exodus According to Women.* New York: Crossroad, 1995.

_____. *The Gospel of Mary: A New Testament for Women.* New York: Crossroad, 1993.

_____. *WomanWisdom: A Feminist Lectionary and Psalter: Women of the Hebrew Scirptures, Part One.* New York: Crossroad, 1991.

_____. *WomanWitness: A Feminist Lectionary and Psalter: Women of the Hebrew Scriptures, Part Two.* New York: Crossroad, 1992.

_____. *WomanWord: A Feminist Lectionary and Psalter: Women of the New Testament.* New York: Crossroad, 1990.

NINE

SEASONS AND EVENTS

Then God said, "Let there be light."
And God saw that the light was good,
and God separated the light from darkness.
God called the light Day and the darkness . . . Night.
And there was evening, and morning, the first day.

—Genesis 1:3–5

When [the Holy One] marked out the foundations of the earth,
then I [Wisdom] was alongside, like a skilled worker. . . .

—Proverbs 8:29–30

THINKING ABOUT HOLY SEASONS

The Christian temporal calendar is founded on two things: the cosmic fact of the earth's relationship with the sun, and the story of the creation of the world in the Jewish scriptures and its retelling in the resurrection of Jesus. These two things gave rise to what is called the temporal calendar: the cycle of commemorations and celebrations of events in the Christian story as keyed to the cycles of the sun. The calendar known as the sanctoral calendar, the commemoration of lives of holy persons, has its roots in the story of Jesus and his holy life, but is keyed to the particular details of each individual story. Historically, both the temporal and sanctoral calendars have focused on the lives and stories of men. A major task of a feminist emancipatory Christian community is to expand this tradition to recall and celebrate the lives of holy women and others who have been neglected, forgotten, distorted, or silenced.

Following the Sun

Human beings tend to want to mark the passage of time. In large part, this impulse to order time is rooted in our experience of the regular natural cycles of the day and month and year, and grows out of our awareness of these cycles. The earth itself marks the passage of time. These natural cycles revolve around the growing and receding of the light. In the case of daily and yearly cycles, it is the sun's light that governs these patterns. The day is marked, at its beginning and at its ending, by the rising and setting of the sun, with the attendant shift from darkness to light and back to darkness again, "marking out the foundations of the earth." The year moves more slowly through a similar pattern of growing and waning daylight. These solar cycles influence not only human behavior, human activity being associated with daylight, rest and sleep with darkness, but these cycles also influence the natural world in which we work and rest. The seasons we know as spring and summer are during the days when the daylight lingers longest in the northern hemisphere, while the seasons of autumn and winter are associated with the shorter days of the opposite turn of the solar year. Plant growth and animal reproduction and ac-

tivity are directly influenced by the fact of the sun's presence and du-
ration and absence in the sky. Likewise, the moon's gravitational
pull, seen through the moon's reflective sunlight, influences the
movement of ocean tides, and the lunar cycles form the basis for the
month and, in turn, the Jewish calendar.

Of course, the invention and ready availability of artificial lighting has weakened our dependence on and therefore our conscious
awareness of these solar and lunar cycles. In a post-Edisonian world,
it is not necessary to cease work when full darkness is upon us, and
we are no longer required to arise with the sun in order to make the
most of the daylight working hours. A flick of a switch and night is
turned into day. Those of us who live in large populated cities and
suburbs may never see the night sky without the effects of artificial
lighting, unless we travel far from our homes and places of work. And
yet, these natural cycles, in their inevitability and their global power
over the natural world in which we live, continue to exert power
over us as well, no matter how artificially removed we may be.

For Jews and Christians, the biblical story of the creation of the
world by the Holy One begins with the separation of light from darkness, as the first act of the creator in bringing order and life out of
chaos. The ordering of night and day, of light and darkness, stands at
the foundation of the world as we know it. Human beings, yes, but
also lives small and large on this planet, are governed by these regular cycles of light and darkness. Even oceans, seas, and rivers respond
to the changing cycles of light and darkness. The work of Wisdom
can be seen in these cycles, Wisdom who was a worker with the Holy
One at the creation of all things. Human imagination has often
tended to place these two powerful realities in opposition to one another, imagining that light and darkness war with one another, strive
for supremacy as if they were armies or enemies. Or human imagination has wanted to see these two powerful realities as complemen-
tary, each unique but the opposite of the other, so that light is never
darkness, darkness never light. But both these imaginings are just
that: imaginings. If one allows oneself to experience the natural
movement from light to darkness to light, without the influence of
artificial lighting, one sees the gradual, nearly imperceptible way that
light and darkness seep into one another. At what moment is it dark

after sunset? At what moment is it light after sunrise? The light grows slowly, the darkness spreads gently. Exact moments of sunrise and sunset can be found in calendars and weather reports, but the experience of these movements makes clear that they are exactly that: movements, gradual and organic. This is Wisdom's work.

It is our human awareness of this powerful force that affected the historical development of religious calendars, including the Christian one. The Jewish calendar is a lunar calendar, following the waxing and waning of the moon's cycles as they affect agriculture. The moon's cycles, of course, are but another form of solar cycle, since it is the reflection of the sun's light appearing through the medium of the moon's movement around the earth that produces them. Although the centuries and their theological disputes overlaid the primitive Christian calendar, at its root it remains a calendar focused on the solar cycles of the year and of the day. Religious observance of the daily cycle is found across religions, including Judaism and Christianity. Morning, with the rising of the sun and growth of daylight, becomes a sign of the faithfulness of the Holy One of Israel, the presence of Wisdom the friend of human beings, and the promise of redemption. The expectation among first-century Jews that the Messiah would appear in the East is a clear expression of this association, as is the ancient practice of facing the east for prayer. The time of sunrise is the messianic time, marked by hope and anticipation. Similarly, early Christians saw in the sun's rising the daily proclamation of the resurrection of Jesus, whom they came to understand to be the Messiah of Israel. It also served as a reminder of the work of creation, in which the first act was the separation of light from darkness. This same light and darkness theme is found in prayer at sundown, where ancient cultural practices associated with lighting evening lamps as the world darkens come to be seen as a reminder of this first act of Creation and of the coming of Jesus, the Wisdom of God, as light in the darkness.

Creation's Time

Where the annual and daily cycles are tied to the sun's disappearance and reappearance, the weekly cycle is tied to the story of creation and its "second chapter" in the story of Jesus' resurrection.

The strong association of Jesus with light, drawn first from messianic themes, is the earliest foundation for the Christian calendar, both daily and annually. Like Wisdom in the book of Proverbs, Jesus as the Word is also said to be with God from the beginning of creation. Jesus as Wisdom's child, or Wisdom's representative, participates in and is revealed by the work of creation, revealed by the separation of light from darkness.

But beyond the daily cycle of light and darkness the earliest Christian timekeeping focused on a nonnatural temporal cycle, that of the week. Whereas the day and the year are founded on solar cycles, and the month on lunar cycles, the week is more or less arbitrary. But the ancient seven-day week, interpreted in Jewish tradition as originating in the story of creation in seven days, provides the temporal framework for telling the Christian story of Jesus' death and resurrection. Common to all gospel stories of the resurrection of Jesus, however they differ in chronological details, is the assertion that Jesus was raised on the first day of the week. It was the Jewish practice to avoid pagan names for the days of the week, since they were taken from names of pagan gods. Instead, they simply numbered the days: first day of the week, second day of the week, and so on. The distinctive day in the Jewish week, of course, is the seventh day, in Hebrew, Sabbath. But Christians, commemorating the resurrection of Jesus, observed the first day as a special day of remembrance and celebration. Early on, this first day of the week is associated with gathering for worship and sharing of the Supper, remembering the resurrection of Jesus as God's emphatic No to suffering.

It is important to notice that the same stories that identify the first day of the week with the resurrection of Jesus also place the women disciples at the center of the story. Consider the biblical evidence:

After the Sabbath, as the first day of the week was dawning, Mary Magdalene and the other Mary went to see the tomb. And suddenly there was a great earthquake; for an angel of the Lord, descending from heaven, came and rolled back the stone and sat upon it. . . . But the angel said to the women, "Do not be afraid; I know that you are looking for Jesus who was crucified. He is not here; for he has been raised, as he

said. Come, see the place where he lay. Then go quickly and
tell his disciples. . . ." (Matt. 28:1–7)

When the Sabbath was over, Mary Magdalene, and Mary the
mother of James, and Salome brought spices so that they
might go and anoint him. And very early on the first day of
the week, when the sun had risen, they went to the tomb.
. . . When they looked up, they saw that the stone, which
was very large, had already been rolled back. As they entered
the tomb, they saw a young man, dressed in a white robe,
sitting on the right side; and they were alarmed. But he said
to them, "Do not be alarmed; you are looking for Jesus of
Nazareth, who was crucified. He has been raised; he is not
here. Look, there is the place they laid him. But go, tell his
[other] disciples and Peter that he is going ahead of you to
Galilee. . . ." (Mark 16:1–7)

But on the first day of the week, at early dawn, they [the
women who came with him to Jerusalem] came to the tomb,
taking the spices that they had prepared. They found the
stone rolled away from the tomb, but when they went in,
they did not find the body. While they were perplexed about
this, suddenly two men in dazzling clothes stood beside
them. The women were terrified and bowed their faces to the
ground, but the men said to them, "Why do you look for the
living among the dead? He is not here, but has risen. . . ."
Then they remembered his words, and returning from the
tomb, they told this to the eleven and all the rest. Now it
was Mary Magdalene, Mary the mother of James, and the
other women with them who told this to the apostles. But
these words seemed to them an idle tale, and they did not believe them. (Luke 24:1–11)

Early on the first day of the week, while it was still dark,
Mary Magdalene came to the tomb and saw that the stone
had been removed from the tomb. . . . But Mary stood weeping outside the tomb. As she wept, she bent over to look
into the tomb; and she saw two angels in white, sitting

where the body of Jesus had been lying, one at the head, the other at the feet. They said to her, "Woman, why are you weeping?" She said to them, "They have taken away my Lord, and I don't know where they have laid him." . . . Jesus said to her, "Mary." She turned and said to him in Hebrew, "Rabbouni!" (which means Teacher). . . . Mary Magdalene went and announced to the disciples, "I have seen the Lord," and she told them that he had said these things to her. (John 20:1, 11–13, 16, 18)

Even though the details of the event vary in the gospels, the constant elements are the presence of the women disciples, always including Mary Magdalene, the occurrence of the event early (at sunrise in three of the four accounts) in the morning of the first day of the week, and the specific instruction to the women to proclaim the resurrection. Sadly, very early in the development of the Christian interpretation of the resurrection story the women's presence is erased or minimized. One early attempt is seen already in the preceding Luke account.

From this brief review of these familiar texts, it is plain that women disciples, and especially Mary Magdalene, stand at the center of the daily observance of the resurrection (at sunrise) and the weekly observance of the resurrection (on the first day of the week). Traditional daily or Sunday liturgies make no reference to this fact. Instead, women's prominence in these commemorations is displaced to an occasional reference in annual commemorations of Holy Week and Easter, and then the women appear only marginally.

What was at first a weekly commemoration of the events of the resurrection on the first day of the week, the day the pagans called Sunday, eventually became a large annual observance, first expanded from a one-day annual vigil to the three holy days, or Triduum Sacrum, and then to the Lenten-Easter-Pentecost season familiar to us. The annual commemoration of this cosmic event also tied the solar cycle with the lunar cycle, as the annual date of Easter is based on the Jewish lunar calendar in which Passover, the time of Jesus' death and resurrection as interpreted by the Gospel writers, falls in the middle of the spring month of Nisan. Thus the human stories of creation of the earth and resurrection of Jesus are ultimately linked with the cosmic reality of the sun's coming and going and its effects on the earth, the moon, and the earth's inhabitants.

Wisdom's work at creation, seen in the rising and setting sun each day and in the waxing and waning sunlight over the course of a month and a year, appears in the humanity of Jesus of Nazareth, Wisdom's child, raised from the dead by the Holy One, witnessed by the women, and testified by Mary Magdalene and the other women disciples. And this central Christian story, the story of the life, ministry, death, and resurrection of Jesus, is written in the cosmic language of the coming and going of the light, that source of all life on earth. Jesus is conceived at the spring equinox, when the light is growing toward the high point of summer's sun. And he is born at the winter solstice, when the darkness is at its deepest, but when the sun's light begins to grow again. And in that light, again at the spring equinox, he is raised from the darkness of death into the growing light of the year. So Christians for centuries have told this story, not only by telling it in words, but also by pointing to the coming and going of the light: "See? The day and the night, the coming and going of the sun's light, all bear witness to the truth of the story!"

Events

In addition to considering the regular cycles of solar and lunar seasons and the cycles of commemorations and celebrations, it is also important for a community to be prepared to observe significant events in the lives of persons in the community. These events fall into three basic categories: life-cycle events, crises, and celebrations, both personal and communal. Life-cycle events include pregnancy, childbirth, first menses, menopause, marriage, leaving home, starting school, graduating, and other moments of importance in one's life. In the case of personal life events, the decision about whether such an event is observed as a private ritual or a communal one rests with the individual. The same rule would apply in the case of occasional events, such as crises or celebrations. Loss or change of job, moving to a new house, changing careers—all are personal or family events that might or might not call for a communal ritual of some sort.

Some events are historical in nature, and their regular remembrance can become part of the common life of a community or family or small group. Such is the case of the commemoration by the "daughters of Israel," who first lamented with the daughter of Jephtha her approaching death and who then returned to the hills every year to hold her in remembrance (the tragic story of Jephtha's daughter is found in Judges 11). A community should be aware of the importance of commemorating similar stories and events and include such in their regular observances. When these events have become part of the community's collective memory and regular cycle of remembrance, they add to the community's cycle of local saints and martyrs.

A SPIRITUAL DISCIPLINE FOR KEEPING TIME

The primal experience of darkness and light is one we deny ourselves too often in our artificially lighted worlds. But greater awareness and attunement to these natural cycles can deepen our understanding of the organic and wise structure of natural time. A regular discipline of attention can help to reorient us (literally). Here are some suggestions.

1. Spend a day and night without artificial light. Make use of sunlight for reading, working, and other daily tasks. Notice how your habits and activities are altered (or not altered) by letting your day and night be directed by natural light. How is the experience different during different times of the year? In winter? In summer?

2. Rise before sunrise (the "exact" time of sunrise will be printed in the weather section of your local newspaper or other local resource). Do not turn on any lights. Sit outside or at a window inside facing the east and watch the sun rise until it is full light. Pray aloud or silently.

3. Stop work or other activities about thirty minutes before sundown (again, the exact time is available through local resources for your location) and sit outside or at a window inside facing the west and watch the sun set until it is full dark. Pray aloud or silently.

4. Go alone or with a group to a wilderness location, as far from major metropolitan areas and their artificial light as possible. Spend at least twenty-four hours away from artificial light, letting your activities be guided by natural light: sunlight, moonlight, starlight, and firelight. Notice the different qualities of the light at different times of day and from different sources.

5. Keep a twelve-month journal of your observations of natural changes in the environment and in you as the seasons change.

PATTERNS FOR HOLY SEASONS:
Creating a Christian Feminist Calendar of Feasts and Fasts

All Christian calendars began as local creations. Christian communities drew on their first-hand experiences of the faith and on the stories they had been told, fusing those experiences and stories with the temporal patterns most familiar to them. Some temporal patterns, as we have seen, have their origin in the natural cycles of day and night, light and darkness, day and year. Some temporal patterns have their origin in ancient stories, stories of creation and of suffering and hope and renewal. Some temporal patterns draw from agricultural cycles of planting, growth, harvest, and rest. The same process is available to contemporary Christian communities as well. The basic Christian calendar starts with the weekly celebration on the first day of the week. On this day, feminist emancipatory communities can create ways of commemorating the central role of women at the resurrection as first witnesses and as first proclaimers of the good news of the resurrection. Since the annual observance of Easter has its origins in this weekly celebration, it is important that the Easter liturgies also restore the central place of the women disciples and witnesses in the telling of the story.

Here is a basic beginning framework for developing your local annual calendar. It takes the solar quarter-days as its starting point and includes the major traditional Christian feast days. As the earliest Jewish calendars began in the spring with the season of new growth, so the earliest Christian calendar began also in spring with Easter. As the Christian calendar evolved over the centuries from this single annual celebration of the heart of the Christian message of hope and life in Jesus' resurrection, the beginning of the year was progressively pushed back earlier and earlier. Our present calendars begin with the season of Advent, because that season was the latest to be added to the calendar, historically speaking. So this calendar, for our purposes, will begin with the spring equinox and the resurrection cycle. But because calendars move in a circle, one may begin anywhere. Rather than seeing the Christian year as a linear progression beginning in Advent and ending at the end of Ordinary Time, it is better to see the year as a cycle that recurs and that can be entered at any point. This keeps us attuned to the natural solar cycle and reminds us that all endings are held within all beginnings.

Using this framework, you can construct your own communal calendar, reflecting your local observances, commemorations, holy people, sacred stories, and natural occurrences. What local persons embody Christ in your community, in your world? Look beyond the famous and well known to those who work quietly, out of the spotlight, perhaps individuals whose lives are known to you or to your community only. Tell their story and remember their names.

What does the change of the day from light to darkness and back into the light again signify where you live? Are there moments or activities that mark these times in ways that are unique to your place in the world? How can these moments or activities be ritualized in recognition of their significance?

What happens where you live when the seasons change? What new things—social, cultural, or natural—mark these changes in the year? Where I live, the departure of Canada geese, flying in long 'V'-formation overhead, calling out, marks a turn in the seasons that is not part of any calendar except that of the geese. The blooming of redbud trees marks another turn toward the light. What natural events mark seasonal turnings that are more local than cosmic in your sacred place? What social or communal events mark changes of seasons in your life? The beginning and ending of school terms? Athletic events? Annual picnics or reunions or homecomings? And what cultural or ethnic observances are important indicators of seasonal changes? Fiestas, commemorations historic and social, fairs and competitions? What identity-confirming celebrations and commemorations mark seasonal movements that give shape and substance to holy seasons in your holy place? The following outline gives a simple framework, with some suggested Christian observations by way of example, following the solar cycles in the northern hemisphere.

Beginning at the spring equinox: (the daylight is equal to the darkness, the daylight is increasing)

March 7: Perpetua and Felicitas, martyrs

March 25: The Annunciation to Mary the mother of Jesus

The Feast of the Resurrection of Jesus/The Feast of the Myrrh-Bearing Women (falling on the first Sunday after the first full moon after the spring equinox)

April 29: Catherine of Siena

May 8: Julian of Norwich

The Feast of the Ascension of Jesus

The Feast of Pentecost

Beginning at the summer solstice: (the daylight is at its longest point; the nighttime is the briefest, but increasing)

July 2: The Visitation of Mary and Elizabeth

July 22: The Feast of Mary Magdalene

July 28: The Feast of Mary and Martha of Bethany

September 17: Hildegard of Bingen

Beginning at the fall equinox: (the daylight is equal to the darkness, the darkness is increasing)

November 20: Mechtilde of Magdeburg

November 22: Cecilia, Martyr

Advent

Beginning at the winter solstice: (the darkness is at its longest point; the daylight the briefest, but increasing)

December 25: The Nativity of Jesus

January 6: The Epiphany

February 1: St. Brigid of Ireland

Patterns for Events

Developing liturgies and prayers for special events draws on patterns for seasons as well as other similar rituals. Life-cycle stages may be compared analogously to nature's seasons or to creation's time. Special events may be celebrative and therefore partake of resurrection themes, or they may be solemn and may resemble Lenten patterns or even mourning rituals associated with death. Transitional events that involve physically moving from one place to another may draw on processional rituals that involve literal movement, accompanied by singing and prayer. Some events may require nothing more elaborate than a blessing and dismissal rite, as modeled in the following section. In every case, liturgies and prayers for events are unique to the individuals involved, their own interpretation of the event being commemorated, and the circumstances in which the event is to take place.

PRAYERS FOR HOLY TIMES AND SEASONS

A PRAYER AT SUNRISE

Holy One, you form light and create darkness.
All creatures in their time
turn toward your light.
Enlighten me this day.
Turn me toward your light,
in peace
in peace
in peace.

A PRAYER AT SUNSET

Holy One, you form light and create darkness.
All creatures in their time
go into the dark with you.
Show me the hidden treasures of darkness
and riches hidden in secret places.
Call me by my name,
in peace
in peace
in peace.

PRAYERS FOR THE QUARTER-DAYS

Spring Equinox

> Day and night are alike to you, Holy One.
> By your Wisdom light and darkness fall into place
> and nourish all that lives.
> Bring me into your holy balance in all things
> and nourish me in your growing light.

Summer Solstice

> Source of all light, Dayspring,
> I lift my face to your light
> and open my lips to your praise
> crying alleluia alleluia
> amen amen.

Fall Equinox

> Night and day are alike to you, Holy One.
> By your Wisdom darkness and light fall into place
> and nourish all that lives.
> Bring me into your holy balance in all things,
> and give me rest in your growing darkness.

Winter Solstice

> Holy One, you form light and create darkness.
> You order the stars and set the planets in their courses.
> The darkness is not dark to you.
> Send me rest in your holy darkness
> and bring me into your growing light.

A Liturgy of Blessing and Dismissal

(This service may be part of or a conclusion to a longer service, perhaps a Sunday service of Word and Table, it may take place apart from a regular gathering of the community, or it may serve as a community worship service in itself.

The person or persons receiving the blessing and dismissal may be invited to come to the center of a circle or to the front of the gathering space. Leaders and community members may stand around or near them. During the movement, music may be played or sung.

Alternatively, if this is a mutual blessing and dismissal (at the last meeting of a class or group, for example, or at the end of a meeting), all may stand in a circle or otherwise facing one another. A song may be sung, if desired.

The designated leader turns to the (first) person to be blessed, and places hands gently on the head, shoulders, or face, as appropriate, in silence. Then the leader says aloud:)

May the Holy One bless you. May you go from here in peace.

(If this is a mutual blessing and dismissal, the person receiving the blessing then may turn to the person next to them and do the same, until all are blessed. Once each one has received blessing and dismissal, that one may leave.

If this is a blessing and dismissal for an individual or small group within the larger community, each person present may bless and dismiss those for whom the liturgy is designed.)

A Liturgy of Holy Darkness

(This service can be held at any time during the waning of the light, between fall equinox and winter solstice, especially leading up to or during Advent. It is best held either in a place that can be artificially darkened or at a time of evening when it is beginning to grow dark.)

God reveals deep and mysterious things,
and knows what is hidden in darkness (Dan. 2:22).

(Quiet instrumental music or chant, preferably wordless)

Genesis 1:1–5 or Isaiah 45:3–7

(Silence)

Psalm 139:1–18

A Meditation on Holy Darkness

(This may be read by one person or printed in full and read by one or more readers, with the community or individuals reading the boldfaced sections.)

Look: the sun's light is waning.
Daylight shortens, night lengthens.
All living creatures of the Northern Hemisphere—
    human creatures, plants, animals, rivers and streams,
        even the very soil itself—
we all draw inward now,
moving into the time when the darkness rises.
Listen:
We lie fallow.
We slow our breathing.
We become dormant, we wait.

The time of holy darkness is God's time.
Even the darkness is not dark to God;
the night is as bright as the day.
It is we living creatures who need the dark:
    its restfulness, the sleep it provides, its embrace.
In the fertile darkness, God creates:
    womb
    egg
    seedling
    root
The living thing, silent and restless, burrows into the
    nurturing dark.
We wait in hope for what will be born.

Christ is conceived at the spring equinox,
to grow in Mary's fertile darkness as the daylight withdraws,
to be born at the darkest time of the year,
moving the world into the light.

The time of holy darkness is full of terror.

Darkness is not for all a time of rest, but a time of fear—
the thief, the murderer, the rapist, the batterer, the abuser—
they all come in the night.
Death comes most often in the darkest hour of night.
The night is full of terror, and God seems to sleep.
The psalmist wishes to flee from God,
but escape is impossible.
God sees in the dark.
And God is everywhere.
The day of the Lord is darkness, and not light.
Perhaps we do well to fear it.
For we cannot hide what we are from God, even in the
	deepest darkness.

The time of holy darkness is a time of revelation.

If we cannot flee from God into darkness, neither can the
	evildoer,
who thinks to hide such deeds from the gaze of God.
Those who think to abuse the vulnerable and exploit those
	in need
imagine that their deeds are covered in darkness.
But the holy darkness of God reveals all.
The day of the Lord is darkness, and not light,
and it reveals all:
the hidden evils that people do,
yes.
And it reveals also the wonders of creation
at work in secret, in the fertile darkness.
Out of it comes
	knowledge and wisdom
	life and light

patience and hope
gift and grace
to all that breathe,
to all that live on the earth.

We live in a time of holy darkness.

We stand poised between chaos and order,
revelation and mystery,
darkness and light.
We imagine, perhaps, that we must choose: dark or light,
chaos or order, clarity or mystery.
But we always live in both, and both are in all things.
The darkness is growing now, but it does not extinguish the
light.
The light will approach, but it is always wrapped in darkness.
And we keep our balance.
At times, the light obscures, and in this time, the darkness
reveals:
knowledge and wisdom
life and light
patience and hope
gift and grace
to all that breathe,
to all that live on the earth.

GREAT THANKSGIVING

May God be with you.

And also with you.

Lift up your hearts.

We lift them up to God.

Let us give thanks to the Holy One, our God.

It is right to give our thanks and praise.

Blessed be your name, Holy One, from age to age,
for wisdom and power are yours.
You change the times and seasons,
you depose the powerful and raise up those who are lowly.
You give wisdom to the wise
and knowledge to those who have understanding.
You reveal deep and hidden things.
You know what is in the darkness, and light dwells with you.
     (Dan. 2:20–23)
To you, O God, we give thanks and praise, joining our voices
     with those who have gone before us into your light, saying:

Holy holy holy
God of blessing and giver of wisdom,
earth, sea, and sky are full of your glory.
Blessings in the highest!
Blessed are all who come in your name.
Blessings in the highest.

Blessed are you, and holy is Jesus, your beloved child,
who grew in the darkness of a womb
and was born into the darkness of the year.

In the evening, before he was betrayed to suffering and death,
Jesus shared a meal with his friends.
He took bread, lifted up his eyes to heaven,
gave you thanks, broke the bread, and gave it to them, saying,
"Take. Eat. This is my body."
After the meal, as the darkness deepened, he took the cup,
lifted up his eyes to heaven and gave you thanks,
and gave them the cup, saying,
"This is my blood of the covenant, which is poured out for
    many.
Truly I tell you, I will never again drink the fruit of the vine
    until I drink it new in the kingdom of God." (Mark 6:41,
    14:22–25)

Remembering Jesus' entry into the darkness,
and awaiting his coming reign,
we offer you these gifts of the earth
and of human labor:
this bread,
this wine,
ourselves.

Pour out your Holy Spirit on us
and on these gifts
that they may be for us
the living presence of Christ.
May we live in Christ's presence
and see the fulfillment of all things.

Through your child Jesus Christ,
in the power of the Holy Spirit,
all honor and glory is yours, Holy One,
now and forever.

Amen.

Blessing

May God be known to us in the night
and quiet the powers of darkness.
May the wisdom of God be our guide
To lead us into peace and safety.

A Great Thanksgiving for Christmas Eve

May God be with you.

And also with you.

Lift up your hearts.

We lift them to our God.

Let us give thanks to the Holy One.

It is right to give our thanks and praise.

We thank you, Holy One,
for you are the creator of darkness and light,
dwelling in silence and known in thunder,
mighty in power and come among us as a helpless infant.

To announce your coming you sent your messengers
to a peasant girl,
to shepherds with their flocks,
to the poor and the homeless.

Therefore, joining our voices with the morning stars
who sang at creation
and the angels and archangels,
and all the beasts of the land,
we sing:

**Holy holy holy
God of blessing and giver of life,
earth, sea, and sky are full of your glory.
Blessings in the highest!
Blessed are all who come in your name.
Blessings in the highest.**

Holy are you, and blessed is your child Jesus Christ,
whose birth we remember this night,
and whose coming again
in justice and peace we await.

On the night before he was betrayed to death,
Jesus sat at supper with his friends.
He took bread, gave you thanks for it,
broke it, and gave it to them, saying,
"Take and eat. This is for you.
Do this in memory of me."

And after supper he took the cup,
gave you thanks,
and gave it to them, saying,
"Take and drink from this, all of you.
This is the new covenant for you and for many
for the forgiveness of sins.
Do this in memory of me."

Remembering, therefore, his birth and his life,
his suffering and death,
his resurrection and ascension,
we offer these gifts of the earth and of human labor:
   this bread,
   this wine,
   ourselves.

Pour out your Holy Spirit on us
and on these gifts of bread and wine
that they may be for us
the living presence of Christ.
May we live in his presence
until the final fulfillment of all things
when all creation will once again
sing and dance for joy.

Through your child Jesus Christ,
in the power of the Holy Spirit,
all honor and glory is yours, Holy One,
now and forever.

Amen.

A FEMINIST EMANCIPATORY SONG OF PRAISE FOR THE PASCHAL LIGHT (*EXSULTET*)

(This may be sung at the Easter vigil at the lighting of the Paschal candle. For a full vigil service, see chapter 10, "Entering into Community.")

Rejoice, rejoice, you heavens!
Let the stars sing aloud
and the clouds proclaim with joy
that fullness has overcome emptiness!

Rejoice and sing, all the round earth,
bright with the glory of heaven,
for light has overcome darkness!

Rejoice, rejoice and sing, communities of hope,
and let your houses shine with light
and ring with the sound of your voices!

All who stand together in the light of this flame,
pray to the Holy One for the grace to sing praises
to the Resurrected One.
Amen.

May God be with you.
And with you too.
Let us give thanks to the Holy One together.
It is good to give thanks.

It is truly right and good
to praise you with heart and mind and body and voice,
and to give thanks for your child Jesus,
who comes to show us your Wisdom
and to rise above the emptiness of death
and lead us into life.

This is the night,
when you brought our ancestors out of slavery in Egypt
and led them through the sea into freedom.

This is the night,
when all who come to you in hope
are delivered from pain and emptiness
and restored to wholeness and fullness of life.

This is the night,
when Christ broke through the bonds of death
and came forth from the grave like a sun.

How wonderful are you, Holy One,
for your mercy to us
in sending your Wisdom
Jesus Christ to open the way for us.

How holy is this night,
when evil takes flight
and oppression ceases;
when the poor of heart enjoy communion with you,
when the mourners find their heart's ease;
when the meek inherit and the hungry are fed;
when the merciful and the pure in heart inherit joy,
and all are peacemakers.

How blessed is this night,
when earth and heaven are joined,
and all earth's inhabitants
are reconciled with you.

Holy One,
receive our evening prayer,
this fire of love and life.
May it shine in the world
in praise of Jesus Christ,
the Morning Star who knows no setting,
our light and our life.
Amen.

A Great Thanksgiving of the Myrrh-Bearing Women: for Easter Day or Season

May God be with you.
And also with you.
Lift up your hearts.
We lift them to our God.
Let us give thanks to God, our Hope.
It is right to give our thanks and praise.

Holy One of Blessing,
in the beginning you created a garden for us
and in the midst of the garden the Tree of Life,
its fruit a sign of your sweetness,
its fragrance a promise of health and wholeness.

Even when we turned our back on your promises,
and made bitter what you created sweet,
you never ceased calling us to yourself
and offering us your peace and wholeness.

By the constant renewal of the earth
and the rebirth of the light through day and year,
you showed your constancy and love.

By your anointed priests and prophets
you spoke to us your words of judgment and of hope.

In the fullness of time you sent Jesus, your Beloved One,
to be born of Mary
and welcomed with wise gifts of beauty, fragrance, and oil,
as signs of a life offering gifts of peace and wholeness to all.

Therefore, together with the renewing earth, with all the
anointed ones sent by you, and with all the joyous company of the faithful who sing before you, we cry out:

Holy holy holy
God of blessing and giver of life,
earth, sea, and sky are full of your glory.
Blessings in the highest!
Blessed are all who come in your name.
Blessings in the highest.

Holy are you, and blessed is Jesus, your Anointed One,
who came to us with words of judgment and hope.

When he suffered and died, faithful women stayed by his side.
When you raised him from the dead,
courageous women came in love
like the magi with an offering of myrrh,
not to Jesus in his swaddling clothes,
but in his winding-sheet.

They came to Christ in tears
but ran forth from his tomb in joy,
announcing his resurrection to all:

Accept the good news of joy from us: Christ has risen!
Exult and celebrate and rejoice, O Jerusalem,
seeing Christ coming from the tomb like a bridegroom!

The night when he was betrayed to death,
Jesus took bread in his hands,
and lifting up his eyes to heaven he gave you thanks
and broke the bread and gave it to them, saying,
"Take and eat. This bread is my body.
Whenever you do this, remember me."

And likewise he took the cup, gave you thanks, and said,
"Drink from this. This is the new covenant in my blood.
Whenever you do this, remember me."

Remembering Jesus, therefore,
and remembering the courageous and faithful women
who anointed him and bear witness to his resurrection
in those days and in our own day,
we offer these gifts of bread and wine and our selves.

Send the power of your strong Spirit
on these gifts and on us who are gathered here.
Fill us with the courage and faith of the myrrh-bearing women

that we may bear witness to the joy and peace of the
    resurrection
and give you praise and thanksgiving
through the anointed and risen One, Jesus Christ,
with your holy and strong Spirit,
now and always.

Amen. Alleluia!

RESOURCES FOR SEASONS AND EVENTS

Black, Kathy, and Heather Murray Elkins, eds. *Wising Up: Ritual Resources for Women of Faith in Their Journey of Aging*. Cleveland: Pilgrim Press, 2005.

Bowe, Barbara, Kathleen Hughes, Sharon Karam, and Carolyn Osiek. *Silent Voices, Sacred Lives: Women's Readings for the Liturgical Year*. Mahwah, N.J.: Paulist Press, 1992.

Henderson, J. Frank. *A Prayer Book for Remembering the Women: Four Seven-Day Cycles of Prayer*. With Hymn Texts by Mary Louise Bringle. Chicago: Liturgy Training Publications, 2001.

_____. *Remembering the Women: Women's Stories from Scripture for Sundays and Festivals*. Chicago: Liturgy Training Publications, 1999.

Litzinger, Sandra Louise. *Word, Wisdom, and Worship: Womanchurch Celebrates the Seasons*. Boulder, Colo.: Woven Word Press, 1999.

Neu, Diann. *Women's Rites: Feminist Liturgies for Life's Journey*. Cleveland: Pilgrim Press, 2003.

Ruether, Rosemary Radford. *Women-Church: Theology and Practice of Feminist Liturgical Communities*. New York: Harper and Row, 1985.

Winter, Miriam Therese. *WomanPrayer, WomanSong: Resources for Ritual*. New York: Meyer Stone/Crossroad, 1987.

TEN

ENTERING INTO COMMUNITY

As many of you as were baptized into Christ
have clothed yourself with Christ.
There is no longer Jew or Greek,
there is no longer slave or free,
there is no longer male or female;
for all of you are one in Christ Jesus.

—Galatians 3:27–28

◈ THINKING ABOUT ENTERING INTO COMMUNITY ◈

We are all members of many different communities, some with overlapping memberships, some quite distinct. A community of family and extended and "honorary" family, a service club community, a civic community, a workplace community, a community of folks who share in our hobbies and avocations, and so on. We often put our church or religious community affiliations in this same general category, as just another community of folks who share interests and pastimes.

But I suggest that the decision to enter into Christian community, especially into emancipatory feminist Christian community, requires great forethought and intentionality, and that the entrance into that community is demanding in ways that we would not normally expect from our other associations, especially our freely chosen associations. In this sense, entering into feminist emancipatory Christian community is more like joining a family than it is like joining a club. Like a family, the feminist emancipatory Christian community may be demanding as well as nurturing, challenging as well as healing. Although Wisdom's house is open and welcoming, it is also not without its expectations, including the expectation that our communities in turn be welcoming.

It is important that the ongoing formation of the lives of members of the feminist emancipatory Christian community be constructed with care and fostered with great intentionality. Here we speak of baptism, but also of other processes of initiation and ongoing nurture. Especially we speak of a feminist emancipatory catechumenate, at the same time a recovery of an ancient Christian practice of preparing persons for baptism, and also a new perspective on an ancient process.

For the first five or six centuries of its history, the church practiced a rigorous initiatory process for those who sought to enter into the Christian community. In a world in which, at some times and in some places, known Christians were subject to harassment, imprisonment, torture, and even death, careful attention to and preparation of Christians was essential. People needed to know what they were getting into, and they needed the support of the community in making that decision. A radical change of life was assumed.

The process that the ancient church developed over time included instructional, disciplinary, and practical elements. Candidates, sometimes called "catechumens," meaning "learners," were subject to a degree of scrutiny by church representatives that we today would find intrusive and alarming; if one's employment, for example, was not consistent with the church's teachings, a candidate was expected to change employment. Candidates were expected to demonstrate Christian charity and love in the care of widows and orphans and those in prison by caring for their physical and spiritual needs. They were expected to engage in regular spiritual disciplines of prayer and worship and to exhibit forgiveness and mercy in their lives. They were expected to attend regular sessions of instruction, especially instruction in the scriptures as well as in the aims and practices of the Christian life. And above all, they were expected to fulfill their role in helping to transform the community further yet into the true body of Christ, in whom there is neither male nor female, Jew nor Greek, slave nor free. In turn, the church community prayed for these candidates and offered them spiritual support during the catechumenal process, as long as it took, which might be as long as three years, and its leaders provided rituals in the form of exorcisms, blessings, and laying on of hands in blessing and dismissal. In every way except participation in the eucharistic meal, catechumens were considered Christians and supported as if they were already full members of the community. And after receiving the water bath of baptism, they were immediately welcomed to the Christian feast of bread and wine and, in honor of their new arrival in the promised land, were also given a cup of milk mixed with honey.

A feminist emancipatory catechumenate will provide structures and processes to aid candidates in the transforming of their lives into the patterns of radical equality professed (although rarely lived up to) by the Christian tradition. This process will include at least these elements:

1. *Claiming power.* For women and other historically subjugated groups, this means learning to claim equality for ourselves, learning how our experiences of oppression differ from and overlap

with the lived oppressions of others, and learning in what ways we have benefited from structures of oppression. For men of the dominant classes, this means learning to stand in solidarity and community with those who are and have been oppressed and are learning to use the benefits of kyriarchal structures to dismantle those structures and bring about radical equality. For all, it means coming to terms with the myriad ways in which power is exercised and experienced, not only in terms of gender and race, but also in terms of class, color, and physical and mental disability. This work of dismantling kyriarchy is not limited to transforming the world outside the community, but also working to transform the community of faith as well, since none of us is immune to the effects of kyriarchal power structures.

2. *Learning the community's story.* Entering into community never takes place in the abstract, but always is a decision to enter into a particular community, with its own history, memories, stories, and practices. The responsibility of introducing candidates into this culture rests with the community itself and its chosen representatives. In the ancient church, candidates had sponsors, individuals who themselves knew the community and its stories intimately and were willing and able to stand with the candidates and support them through the demanding process. Some such arrangement is the best way to provide this communal support, to create or strengthen bonds between candidates and the community, and to prevent the development of an internal class system of elites and newcomers. It is assumed, of course, that the feminist emancipatory community is already engaged in the work of recovering the lost, distorted, and forgotten stories of subjugated peoples, both in the larger history of Christianity and in the world.

3. *Engaging in emancipatory works.* The Christian life includes, at its heart, practices that work to transform the world. Candidates for entering the community should be guided in choosing a specific local context in which to do this emancipatory work. It may be that a work already undertaken by the local community will provide a suitable location for this work, or it may be that a

candidate brings to the process interests, passions, and commitments that can open the community to new places to work for the transformation of the world. This can be one of the places that the candidates help to transform the community into which they enter.

4. *Engaging in emancipatory spiritual disciplines.* For persons coming into feminist emancipatory community, disciplines that can free the imagination from kyriarchal restrictions will be both helpful and perhaps challenging. Learning to name the Holy One as female, as not white, as poor, as one of us, as not human, and in myriad other ways can be difficult without the support and example of a community that knows how to do this and supportive individuals with whom to share one's struggles.

In addition to these practices, communities may discover others that will further the transformation of church and world, and support individuals and communities in this work.

The ancient baptismal rites themselves were likewise rich, complex, and fully physical. Candidates for baptism were not permitted to witness, let alone partake in, the communion ritual before they received baptism. Likewise, none of the lengthy instruction included any information about the baptismal event, and candidates were also not permitted to witness the baptism of others. Once they came to the event itself, therefore, they were undoubtedly anxious, excited, and ready to be amazed. And in fact, the first instruction they received upon entering the place where the large baptismal pool was located was to take off their clothes. Besides the candidates themselves, only the presider (normally the bishop) and the assisting deacons and deaconesses were present. Candidates were asked to face the west and renounce evil and turn to the east and declare for Christ. Then, one by one, they were anointed over the whole body with perfumed oil, led into the pool, and dunked under the water three times as they were asked the Trinitarian questions: "Do you believe in God?" "Do you believe in Jesus?" "Do you believe in the Holy Spirit?" Upon coming up out of the pool they were clothed again, received from the bishop a laying on of hands and another anointing on the head, and then were led out to the nearby church where the gathered community welcomed them to their first communion meal. For all of its patriarchal trappings of hierarchy, this was a richly physical and sensuous experience that seems at the same time shocking and attractive to us, who are familiar only with the most minimal baptismal liturgies, with little drama, little water, and little power.

A feminist emancipatory baptism needs to reclaim the power of this richly physical experience while reshaping its hierarchical elements into signs of radical equality. Indeed, the earliest Christian testimony to the meaning of baptism insists on this social equality: "As many of you as were baptized into Christ have clothed yourself with Christ. There is no longer Jew or Greek, there is no longer slave or free, there is no longer male or female; for all of you are one in Christ Jesus" (Gal. 3:27–28). Much of the church's history is the story of its attempts to live up to this standard and its many failures to do so. The challenge for emancipatory feminist baptismal practice, therefore, is first to work at making the baptized community into which new members are welcomed as egalitarian a community as possible.

A SPIRITUAL DISCIPLINE FOR ENTERING INTO COMMUNITY: Developing a Feminist Emancipatory Cathecumate

A community intending to welcome new members into its midst must undertake a serious process of discernment in order to develop a healthy, useful, and transformative catechumenate that will benefit both the candidates and the community. This process of discernment might follow the feminist pathways with a view toward creating an emancipatory catechumenal process.

What is the wisdom of our common life?

This invites the community to review its story as a community, to consider the ways it has lived out emancipatory freedom within itself and in relation to the world around it. What are the key stories that show this? How has this community failed to live out this freedom? Recognition of failures and weaknesses is necessary not only for the community's self-critical self-understanding, but also as an important element in welcoming new members. It is not healthy to pretend that any community is perfect, and by naming weaknesses and failures catechumens are invited into deeper self-examination and greater involvement in bringing the community closer to its own aims.

What is the wisdom of our bodies?

This question invites the community to consider the ways in which it attends to our physical lives and well-being, both within the community and in the world at large. How do we support one another in caring for our bodies? How do we provide for the physical well-being of others in the world? How does this bodily care extend beyond care for human bodies to care for all that lives, for the earth, for the water, for the air we breathe?

What is the wisdom of our suffering and struggle?

Here the community can review the struggles and suffering of its own members, of the community as a whole, and of all subjugated and oppressed communities around the world. What have we learned? What are we still learning? How can the catechumenal process best draw on this wisdom?

What is the wisdom of our relationships?

What have we learned as an emancipatory community that we can offer to those seeking to enter into the community? How have we negotiated our complex relationships across race, gender, ethnicity, age, class, and ability? How have we modeled feminist emancipatory relationships in the world and in our encounters with others? What do catechumens have to teach us about relationships? How do we welcome inquirers and guests and those who are newly entering into the community? How do we welcome children who are presented for baptism or blessing in the community? How are their gifts and presence received and celebrated? What have we learned from them?

PATTERNS FOR ENTERING INTO COMMUNITY

A Feminist Emancipatory Catechumenate

Feminist emancipatory catechesis will normally proceed in stages, but pastoral decisions about adjusting the stages for individuals may be made in consultation with the candidate(s), the sponsor(s), the community's leaders (particularly those charged with directing the catechumenal process), and, where reasonable, the community as a whole.

1. *Inquiry.* The first step is when an individual (or group) inquires about coming into the community, perhaps on the basis of familiarity or kinship with someone who is already a member, perhaps because of getting to know the community's work, perhaps because they are seeking an open emancipatory community for living out their Christian life. In the spirit of Wisdom's house, they should be made welcome and encouraged in their search. Each community will develop its own processes for responding to inquiries, and, as long as these processes are welcoming, local variations that recognize the unique contexts of each community are appropriate. At the most basic level, someone should be prepared to answer any questions that an inquirer might have about the process of entering the community, about the expectations for being a member of the community, and about its regular common life.

2. *Welcome as catechumens.* When the inquirer and those responsible for directing the catechumenal process are satisfied that everyone wishes to proceed, the candidate(s) may be introduced to the whole community as part of a regular gathering for worship. An example of a welcoming rite is found below: "Welcome to Wisdom's house."

3. *Participation in feminist emancipatory catechumenate.* The length of this period of instruction and preparation will be determined by the needs and intentions of the community as well as the pastoral needs of each candidate. The core of the catechumenate might be an established period of instruction coupled with a pe-

riod of intensive attention to spiritual disciplines, including external as well as internal practices, of indeterminate length. This work might best be undertaken in partnership with a member of the community, a sponsor, perhaps, or spiritual director.

4. *Decision to ask for baptism and/or membership in the community.* Normatively, this process presupposes adult candidates, or at least persons old enough to make serious decisions for their own lives. Parents of young children or infants must be prepared to make this request with full awareness of the seriousness of the commitment involved, on their part as well as for their children.

5. *Participation in the rites of baptism and membership.* Although the rites of baptism and membership are most powerfully manifested at the Easter celebration, there can be sound reasons for a community to have baptismal rites at other times of the year. Whenever the rites are held, due attention should be given to the relationship between the rites and the seasons, in order to make the most effective and meaningful use of natural cycles.

A Feminist Emancipatory Baptismal Rite

A full baptismal service includes four basic elements. Each of these elements includes several actions as well. The service should be expected to take at least two hours or more, depending on decisions about the number of readings and the number of baptizands. When this takes place during the Easter celebration, the Easter Vigil, with its powerful use of natural daily cycles of light and darkness and of the solar cycle of the spring equinox, provides an especially fitting time for this event. The four service sections noted here presume the context of the Easter Vigil, beginning in darkness before sunrise and moving into the eucharist when the sun is up.

1. *The Service of Light:* When the service begins in darkness, this portion consists of the lighting of the Christ candle from a new fire and a sung greeting to the light (traditionally, this is the *Exsultet*, available in many resources in English translation and with chant tones), which is carried into the gathering space from the fire outside.

2. *The Service of the Word:* This portion is a classical vigil, with a sequence of scripture reading, psalm or hymn, and prayer. The number of readings may vary, but the Easter Vigil traditionally has included the creation story, the crossing of the Red Sea, the entry into the promised land, and the New Testament account of the resurrection of Jesus. It also may include a sermon or other form of scriptural interpretation.

3. *The Service of Baptism:* This portion of the service itself includes several elements:
   a. Presentation of candidates for baptism and/or baptismal renewal
   b. Renunciation of sin and evil, and declaration of adherence to Christ
   c. Baptism in water, with laying-on of hands and anointing with oil
   d. Acclamation of welcome by the community; this may include giving each newly baptized person a white garment, shawl, or stole, and/or a lighted candle.

4. *The Service of the Table:* This portion of the service includes preparation of the table, the praying of the Great Thanksgiving, and the sharing of communion, with the newly baptized receiving communion first, including a special cup of milk mixed with honey.

PRAYERS FOR ENTERING INTO COMMUNITY

WELCOME TO WISDOM'S HOUSE

(This may take place at the beginning of the regular gathering for worship, or at some other point in the service as appropriate. The candidate(s) may gather at the entrance to the worship space. The community may turn, if necessary, to face the entrance. The candidate(s) knock on the door or doorway.)

LEADER: Who seeks to enter Wisdom's house?

CANDIDATES: (*call out their first names*)

LEADER: (*Names*), what do you ask of us?

CANDIDATES: To be welcome in Wisdom's house.

ALL: Be welcome, in the name of the Holy One!

(The candidate(s) may enter and may be embraced or otherwise made welcome in the midst of the community.)

LEADER: We welcome you into this community as a seeker (as seekers) after Wisdom. We promise to support you and to pray for you as you prepare yourself (yourselves) for entry into this community.

(The leader lays hands on each candidate and offers this blessing:)

May Wisdom guide your feet,
open your heart, and
enlighten your mind.

(The catechumen(s) are prayed for by name in the intercessions each time the community gathers for worship. They may also be invited forward or into the midst of the community at the end of the gathering for worship for laying-on of hands and blessing.)

A LITURGY OF EMANCIPATORY BAPTISM
AT THE EASTER VIGIL

(The service begins in the dark, ideally so that the entire service concludes as the sun rises. There should be present in some form a large body of water, large enough for the baptizand(s) and the person performing the baptism to enter the water. A portable hot tub, large watering trough such as are available at farm supply stores, or a natural body of water would be suitable, depending on the space in which the community gathers.)

The Service of Light

(The community, including the catechumen(s), gathers outdoors around a fire pit where a fire has been laid ready. A leader strikes new fire from a flint until a spark catches the prepared fire. While the fire burns, the community may sing or chant or watch in silence. When the fire is burning well, a leader lights a large tall candle directly from the new fire, lifts it high, and says or sings:)

The Light of Hope!

PEOPLE: **Amen!**

(Here individuals may greet the light, naming it as they choose: Light of Life, Light of Wisdom, etc., and all respond "Amen!" Concluding this, the leader announces:)

The Light of Christ!

PEOPLE: **Amen!**

(The people may then process dancing into the gathering space, singing, or moving to instrumental music or drumming.)

The Service of the Word

(The service of readings, songs, and prayers follows, with individuals from the community reading the texts—from Jewish and Christian scriptures, and/or other sources as appropriate—leading the songs or psalms, and offering the prayers. If desired, a leader or other designated member of the community may offer reflections on the readings and/or the occasion, or there may be general discussion, or silence. If part of the Easter Vigil, the readings would normally conclude with the reading of one of the resurrection narratives from the Synoptic Gospels that makes clear the presence of women at the tomb.)

The Service of Baptism

(When this service of the word is completed, the community may process or dance to the water, singing or moving to instrumental music or drumming. The catechumens, their sponsors, and the persons charged with leading the baptism take their places near the pool, with the rest of the congregation gathered in a circle around them.)

The Promises

(The leader invites each catechumen, each candidate for membership, or parent of a child too young to answer for itself to renounce evil and to declare their faith before the community. Each is given no more than two minutes to speak.)

The Baptism

(One at a time, each catechumen enters the water, led in by the sponsor and received by the person designated to perform the baptism. The baptizer may pour water over each person's head or, placing one hand on the person's mouth and nose, let each down gently face-first into the water three times. Each time, the baptizer may ask:)

Do you believe in God, the Holy One?

BAPTIZAND: I believe.

BAPTIZER: Do you believe in Jesus, Mary's child, Wisdom's prophet?

BAPTIZAND: I believe.

BAPTIZER: Do you believe in the Spirit?

BAPTIZAND: I believe.

(As each newly baptized person is led out of the water, each is welcomed by her or his sponsor, who offers a large towel or warm shawl that is wrapped around the newly baptized. After all have been through the water, the newly baptized and the candidates for membership draw together for the anointing.)

The Anointing

(A member of the community reads Mark 14:1–9 or Matthew 26:1–13, the story of the woman who anoints Jesus' head before his death. Following this reading, a woman in the community (or more than one, if the numbers warrant it) comes forward and anoints each catechumen and candi-

date for membership with perfumed oil. This may be done by marking the forehead, rubbing the oil on the face or on the hands, or pouring the oil over the head. The use of oil should be generous, and ample time taken with the gesture. There may be singing during this act, or it may be done in silence.)

The Welcome
(Each sponsor now steps forward and presents the newly baptized and the new members to the congregation by name: "I present our new member, (Name)! Welcome her/him to Wisdom's Table!" The whole community then processes or dances to the space prepared for the eucharist.)

The Service of the Table
(The eucharist proceeds as usual, with provision for the new members to receive communion first, and to receive a drink from a Welcome Cup of milk mixed with honey.)

RESOURCES FOR ENTERING INTO COMMUNITY

Paulsell, Stephanie. *Honoring the Body: Meditations on a Christian Practice*. San Francisco: Jossey-Bass, 2002.

Procter-Smith, Marjorie. *In Her Own Rite: Constructing Feminist Liturgical Tradition*. Akron, Ohio: OSL Publications, 2000.

Ruether, Rosemary Radford. *Women-Church: Theology and Practice of Feminist Liturgical Communities*. New York: Harper and Row, 1985.

ELEVEN

MEALS

(Wisdom) has slaughtered her animals,

she has mixed her wine,

she has set her table . . .

"Come, eat of my bread, and drink of the wine I have mixed."

—Proverbs 9:5

THINKING ABOUT MEALS

To live we must eat. At the most fundamental level, this action of eating is biologically compelled, and it is a need that we share with all other living things. Plants, animals, insects, birds—all that live must take in food in order to grow and continue to live. To eat is to participate in a cycle of life and death. In order for animals to eat, something else must die. This deep connection between life and death, and therefore between the living and the dead, is the basis for all religious interpretations of food and meals, and it accounts, at least in part, for the presence of ritual meals and special food in virtually every religion.

At the same time, in the industrialized West, we are far removed from this deep connection, preferring to assume that the meats and grains and vegetables and fruits we consume appear bloodlessly and harmlessly on our plates or in our supermarkets. By ignoring or denying the death that is required for us to eat, we miss this vital connection, both in our ordinary daily meals and in our religious meals. We are faintly embarrassed, perhaps, or even shocked, that Wisdom boldly announces that she has "slaughtered her animals" for her feast.

Culturally, the production and serving of meals has often fallen to those whose social standing is marginal: women, children, slaves, persons whose skin color, class, education level, or mental ability are deemed lesser than that of the ruling or dominating classes. If Wisdom is presented in the scriptures as an educated and perhaps upper-class woman, we should also be shocked and surprised that she slaughters her animals, sets her table, and prepares her feast with her own hands, without relying on the subjugated labor of others. Meals in Wisdom's house are emancipatory meals.

In the New Testament, Jesus too is depicted as violating many meal traditions and taboos. He famously eats with sinners, tax collectors, and other outsiders, scandalizing his more proper and religiously observant witnesses. He particularly is shown at meals with women, in their houses, and praises Mary's choice to study with him over Martha's choice of women's traditional role of meal preparation.

At the same time, it is important to recognize that women's traditional presence at meal preparation and service means that they were much more present and involved in all domestic meal scenes than is represented in the New Testament. Of particular importance is women's undoubted presence at Jesus' meal with his disciples in the upper room before his death, the text's silence about women's presence notwithstanding. Then as in many parts of the world now, primary responsibility for meal preparation and serving rests with women. They are often invisible to the male diners, since they often labor out of sight and in some contexts do not sit down at table and dine with others.

Jesus tells many stories about meals: wedding feasts and banquets are common elements in the parables, where they often serve as a model for the messianic age. "A king gave a wedding banquet for his son"; "Many will come from east and west and will eat with Abraham and Isaac and Jacob in the kingdom of heaven"; "Someone gave a great dinner, and invited many." This image of the elaborate feast, the banquet to which many are invited, finds expression in the related stories of miraculous feedings. A large crowd gathers to hear Jesus speak or to seek healing from him. Evening comes, and the large crowd has no food. They are hungry. And Jesus takes a few fish, some loaves of bread, gives the Holy One thanks for it, breaks the bread and shares it with all, and everyone is fed, with food left over. This is the very image of the messianic banquet, that generous heavenly meal, made present to tired and hungry people. This image of the absurd generosity of God resonates throughout the New Testament and echoes in the Christian meal called eucharist, "thanksgiving."

Meals create and sustain community. The loss of time spent preparing meals and sitting down to eat together is often lamented, and the price paid for convenient, fast food on the go is obesity and lack of community. The meal stories in the New Testament make clear the power inherent in shared meals by reminding us of the importance of who is invited and who is not, how the meals are prepared and how guests are welcomed, what is eaten and how we eat together. And when meals are shared in an open-handed way, the messianic community is manifested, and all are fed, and there is enough and more than enough.

Jesus' meals with disciples do not end with his death, even though we often call the meal in the upper room "the Last Supper." It wasn't. The Resurrected One shares meals with his disciples two times in the New Testament. The Gospel of Luke describes two disciples walking the road to Emmaus, lamenting Jesus' death, when they are joined by a stranger who explains the meaning of these tragic events to them. They invite him to join them for supper, and at supper they recognize the Resurrected One at last, "in the breaking of the bread." In John's Gospel we learn of another gathering of despondent disciples, this time Peter and several others who had made a living fishing, going out early to fish on the Sea of Tiberias. When they return from their unsuccessful fishing trip, a stranger on the shore advises that they cast their nets again. And drawing up a vast catch, they at last recognize the Resurrected One. Jesus cooks fish for them over a fire, breaks bread, and gives it to them, and they are fed.

It would seem that Jesus, in life and in resurrected Life, is the One who feeds us, who is in fact present to us in our hunger and in our satisfying our hunger, in our need for bread, and in our sharing of bread with one another. Although this simple fact has been, at various times in the church's history, more or less elaborated, ritualized, and enacted, it is at its heart a meal, which is a response to human hunger for food and for community.

A SPIRITUAL DISCIPLINE OF MEALS

1. *Eat simply.* By eating simple, minimally processed, and naturally grown food, we can recover the pleasures of food and eating.

2. *Eat in season.* Food is grown and harvested according to natural local cycles. Learn to enjoy food in season, rather than expecting to eat anything at any time of the year. This practice helps link us to seasons and to the earth's cycles.

3. *Eat locally.* Locally grown food is tied to the growing seasons, so it is another form of eating in season. But by eating locally, we also support the labor of people in our communities. Thus the communion of saints present at our dinner table includes our neighbors, represented by food they have grown. Eating locally also saves fossil fuels used to transport food over long distances and limits pollution produced by burning fossil fuel in transportation. And the food tastes better!

4. *Raise food to eat.* This can be as simple as a pot with a tomato plant or herb in it, or as elaborate as a vegetable garden or greenhouse. For communities who wish to take on this spiritual discipline, community gardens are often available in most cities. People in communities with members who own farms or sufficient property to support a garden can provide labor in exchange for a portion of the harvest. This is the best spiritual discipline of food. It links us with natural growing cycles of sun, moon, and seasons, links us with the earth on which we live, and provides us with the fullest possible appreciation and understanding of the combination of human labor and nature's gifts.

5. *Eat mindfully.* Begin each meal in prayer or silent meditation, giving thanks for the food and recognizing the combination of divine gift and human labor that produces it. Eat slowly and reflectively.

6. *Set aside one day a week to gather around the table for a meal.* This might be done by a group of friends, a family, or a group within the worshiping community. Let all cooperate in preparing the

food, setting the table, and cleaning up after the meal. Choose food that does not depend on subjugated labor. This meal might include one of the meal blessing rituals in the "Prayers" section in this chapter.

7. *Prepare bread for use in one's regular meals, gathering meals, or eucharistic meals.* The process of making bread serves to remind us, in a physical way, of the centrality and power of bread in our lives and in the Christian tradition.

PATTERNS FOR MEALS

Meals have their own rituals, aside from religious reinterpretations. These basic patterns involve planning the meal, buying or harvesting the food, preparing the food, preparing the table, sharing the food, eating, and cleaning up after eating, which may involve storing or distributing leftover food. During the whole process, particularly when meals involve a group, conversation and stories provide narrative content to the meal process. In religious contexts, such as the Shabbat meal or Passover meal in Judaism or the eucharist in Christianity, conversation and narrative often take center stage, providing a kind of commentary on the meaning of the food and of the meal itself. But this is often true as well of family meal gatherings, especially at events of high significance, such as wedding meals, birthday celebrations, and Thanksgiving, Christmas, and Easter meals. Traditional foods are eaten, memories recalled, stories told, and the common narrative of the group taken up again for a new generation. This process renews the family's sense of identity and helps to initiate new family members into this particular communal narrative stream.

Here are some suggestions for meal patterns and shapes, based on biblical meal stories.

Wisdom's Feast

This meal is based on Proverbs 9:1–6, in which Wisdom invites all who would learn of her to her table. Invite friends, coworkers, neighbors. Let all who are dining gather and prepare simple, whole, fresh, and beautiful food of the season. Invite everyone to bring a favorite bowl, plate, serving platter, cups, glassware, table linens, silverware, flowers, candles, etc. All help set the table(s) and prepare the food; all serve one another. If desired and appropriate, the meal may begin with the Great Thanksgiving of Holy Wisdom (in the following "Prayers" section) and the sharing of bread and wine. The meal may then follow. During the meal tell stories of memorable meals and of favorite foods and dishes; remember those who are absent, especially those who have died, both locally and globally. Remember those who raised and harvested the food.

Messiah's Table

Based on New Testament parables of Jesus about the messianic banquet in Matthew 8:11–12 and 22:1–14; Luke 13:29 and 14:13–24, this meal places the focus on justice. In the messianic feast texts, Jesus cautions against presuming that one's religious observances or status will get one into the messianic community. Therefore we prepare for this meal by first examining ourselves for such presumptions, and we open ourselves to the possibilities of messianic communities beyond our own communities. It might be most fitting to invite those who lack justice in their lives or in the world to this feast and to make them the honored guests. If appropriate, the meal may begin with the Great Thanksgiving of the Messianic Banquet (in the following "Prayers" section) and sharing of bread and wine. The meal may follow, with companionable sharing of stories.

Miraculous feeding

This is a meal of generosity. Based on the miraculous feeding stories of the New Testament found in Mark 6:34–44 and John 6:1–14, this meal feeds the hungry. It should be planned in concert with an organization that is authorized to distribute food to the homeless and the hungry in your city or town. The same quality of food that would be part of a feast in the community should be provided, prepared with the same care and attention and in a spirit of generosity.

Resurrection feast

Based on the post-resurrection meals with Jesus found in the New Testament in Luke and in John, this is a meal of recognition. The food should be very simple, perhaps simply bread and wine or fruit juice, fish, cheese, olives, or other simple fare. The meal may begin with the Great Thanksgiving of Wisdom the Worker (in the following "Prayers" section), or a simple prayer of blessing (of the sort provided in the "Prayers" section). While the simple food is shared, the participants may meditate in silence, share stories about when and how they have recognized Jesus the Resurrected One in their lives, or take it in turn to read from one or more of the biblical accounts of Jesus' resurrection appearances (Matt. 28:1–20; Mark 16:1–20; Luke 24:1–53; John 20:1–21:25).

Word and Table

The combination of a service of the Word, focusing on the reading and interpretation of scripture, with a service of the Table occurred very early in Christian practice. This is a meal of companionship and presence. The community gathers to hear the Word proclaimed and to share in its interpretation, as discussed in chapter 8, "Speaking and Listening to the Holy: Scripture." This service might take place in a room that accommodates everyone seated facing one another, perhaps with a desk of some sort to hold a book for reading. When this service is completed, the community may gather around a table, perhaps in another space or another part of the gathering space, to pray together, giving thanks for bread and wine and for the gift of companionship with the Holy One. This prayer would normally take the form of the Great Thanksgiving, and it can be written, adapted, or selected to make it suitable for the occasion.

Prayer Patterns for Meals

The church's eucharistic prayer, also known as the Great Thanksgiving, has, over the centuries, become mystified and hedged about with hierarchical restrictions of various kinds. One of the chief restrictions in most of the church's history, and still in effect in many Christian communities, is against women speaking this prayer. Other restrictions have included race, educational level, sexual orientation, and physical ability.

But at its heart, this prayer is simply an expanded and adapted version of a traditional Jewish meal prayer: a blessing over bread and wine. At Wisdom's open table, surely anyone who is able to speak the words in the midst of the community, and to whose words the community is willing to confirm with their "amen," is capable of praying this prayer.

The form itself is simple. A simple meal prayer (often known by its Hebrew opening word, *berakah*, or "blessing") follows this pattern:

1. Blessing of God: "Blessed be the Holy One" or "Blessed are you, Holy One"

2. Action of God: "who brings forth food from the earth" or "you bring forth food from the earth"

3. Remembering and request (optional): "You have fed us bountifully; now bless this food"

4. A concluding blessing or word of praise: "Blessed are you, Holy One"

The Great Thanksgiving, or Eucharistic Prayer, expands this simple form, often following this pattern:

1. Opening dialog: Here the leader greets the community and they respond, affirming the leader's authority to pray on their behalf and in their midst.

2. Thanksgiving: Here thanks and blessings to the Holy One for all gifts or gifts specifically related to the occasion are offered. This thanksgiving may include a version of the traditional "Holy Holy Holy" (*sanctus*) and "blessed is the one who comes" (*benedictus qui venit*) as congregational song.

3. Remembrance: Here the work of Jesus and specifically the words of Jesus at his last meal before his death are recalled. Other meals of Jesus may also be recalled here.

4. Offering: Here the community's common life, represented in the bread and wine, is offered as gift in return for all of the gifts of the Holy One. Here the reciprocal exchange occurs: we offer as gift back to the One who has first given these gifts to us.

5. Closing word of praise: Here the original thanksgiving is summed up and proclaimed.

6. Community Amen: Here the congregation confirms the leader's words of prayer and thanksgiving.

PRAYERS FOR MEALS

A MEAL PRAYER OF BLESSING
(This prayer may be said at the beginning or at the conclusion of a meal.)

Blessed are you, Holy One.
You bring forth food from the earth
and by your hand we are fed.
For this food we give thanks.
For the labor that produced this food we give thanks.
For the hands that prepared this food we give thanks.
For our hunger that you feed we give thanks.
Blessed are you, Holy One.

A MEAL PRAYER ADDRESSED TO JESUS
(This prayer may be said at the beginning of a meal, especially if the meal begins with breaking and sharing bread.)

Bread of Heaven,
Cup of Salvation,
River of Living Water,
Light of the World,
from you comes every good gift
and to you we turn in our hunger.
Have mercy on us,
feed us with the words of life,
and be known to us in the breaking of this bread.

Great Thanksgiving of Holy Wisdom

Wisdom has slaughtered her animals,
she has mixed her wine,
she has also set her table.
She has sent out her women ministers.
She calls from the high places,
"Come, eat of my bread,
drink of the wine I have mixed.
Lay aside immaturity and live,
and walk in the way of insight."

May God be with you.
And with you too.
Lift up your hearts.
We lift them to the Holy One.
Let us give thanks to God in this place.
It is good to give thanks together.

Holy One of Wisdom,
we give you thanks for bringing us together in this place.
You established the foundations of the earth,
and set the boundaries of the sea.
Your wisdom upholds the world,
your path leads to understanding.
All earth's creatures are in your care,
and you delight in your human children.

Even when we have turned away from your pathways
you have come after us, searching the streets
and calling us to your banquet table.

And so, with all your creation
and your prophets of every age, we sing:

Holy holy holy
God of blessing and giver of wisdom,
earth, sea, and sky are full of your beauty.
Blessings in the highest!
Blessed are all who come in your name.
Blessings in the highest.

Holy are you, and blessed is your prophet Jesus,
Child of Mary, friend of humankind.
He traveled by your paths and taught your wisdom to all.
Poor himself, to the poor he offered hope;
oppressed unto death, to the oppressed he announced
        freedom.

The night when he was betrayed to death,
Jesus your prophet once again called the wise to your table
and took bread in his hands.
Lifting up his eyes to heaven he gave you thanks
and broke the bread and gave it to them, saying,
"Take and eat. This bread is my body.
Whenever you do this remember me."
Come, eat of my bread.
And after the meal he took the cup, gave you thanks,
        and said,
"Drink from this. This is the new covenant in my blood.
Whenever you do this, remember me."
Come, drink of the wine I have mixed.

Remembering Jesus, therefore,
we offer these gifts of bread and wine and our selves
in the midst of this holy gathering.

Send the power of your strong Spirit
on these gifts and on us gathered in this holy place.

Make this meal, this place, and this people
holy and blessed, true signs of your presence in the world.
Come, Holy Wisdom, build your house in this place.
Through your prophet Jesus Christ,
in your holy and strong Spirit
in this holy gathering,
now and always.
Amen.

C

GREAT THANKSGIVING OF HOLY WISDOM THE WORKER

May God be with you.
And also with you.
Lift up your hearts.
We lift them to our God.
Let us give thanks to God our Light.
It is right to give our thanks and praise.

Holy One of Blessing,
at the beginning of your work
you created Holy Wisdom, an image of your goodness,
bringing her forth for your delight.
With her at your right hand you brought forth the deeps
and pulled up the mountains;
you called out the springs of water
and set the foundations of the earth.

And Holy Wisdom was beside you as a skilled worker,
rejoicing in creation and delighting in the human race.

Even when we turned our back on your deep knowledge,
and sought simple answers and easy solutions,
you never ceased calling us to yourself,
offering your wisdom and enlightenment.
In every generation Holy Wisdom comes among us
passing into holy souls,
seeking to make us your friends and her prophets.

Therefore, together with all creation,
with Holy Wisdom herself,
and all her prophets of all times, we cry out:

Holy holy holy
God of blessing and giver of wisdom,
earth, sea, and sky are full of your glory.
Blessings in the highest!
Blessed are all who come in your name.
Blessings in the highest!

Holy are you, and blessed is Jesus, your Wisdom,
born of Mary,
who came to us with words of judgment and hope,
whose yoke is easy, and whose burden is light.

The night when he was betrayed to death,
Jesus took bread in his hands,
and lifting up his eyes to heaven he gave you thanks
and broke the bread and gave it to his friends, saying,
"Take and eat. This bread is my body.
Whenever you do this, remember me."

And likewise he took the cup, gave you thanks, and said,
"Drink from this. This is the new covenant in my blood.
Whenever you do this, remember me."

Remembering Jesus, therefore,
and remembering all who do Wisdom's work,
we offer these gifts of bread and wine and our selves.

Send the power of your strong Spirit
on these gifts and on us who are gathered here
that we may know your wisdom
and give you praise and thanksgiving
through your Wisdom Jesus Christ,
with your holy and strong Spirit,
now and always.

Amen.

ℭ

GREAT THANKSGIVING OF
THE MESSIANIC BANQUET

May God be with you.
And also with you.
Lift up your hearts.
We lift our hearts to God.
Let us give thanks to the Holy One.
It is right to give our thanks and praise.

We give you thanks and praise, Holy One,
for you are the bountiful giver of all good gifts.
You placed us in the garden
and provided us with every green plant for food.
Although we rejected your bounty,
you called us again and again to your table of reconciliation
    and grace.

From the beginning you sent your Wisdom among us;
she sought us out and befriended us,
setting a rich table before us
and calling us to come and learn her ways.
You open your hand,
and we are filled with good things;
you send forth your spirit,
and we are renewed.

And so, with all your people on earth
and all the company of heaven,
we praise your name and join their unending hymn:

Holy holy holy
God of blessing and giver of wisdom,
earth, sea, and sky are full of your glory.
Blessings in the highest!
Blessed are all who come in your name.
Blessings in the highest!

Holy are you, and blessed is your Wisdom, Jesus Christ,
who came among us to teach us your ways
and call us to your great feast.
He first showed forth your glory at a wedding feast,
making water into wine;
he fed the hungry multitudes,
making a small meal into a great feast.
he shared meals with sinners and outcasts,
showing us the wideness of your table.

On the night before he was betrayed to death,
he sat at a meal with his friends.
He took bread, gave thanks to you, broke the bread,
and gave it to his friends, saying,

"Take, eat; this is my body which is given for you.
Do this in remembrance of me."

When supper was over, he took the cup,
gave thanks to you, and gave it to his friends, saying,
"Drink from this, all of you;
this is the blood of the new covenant,
poured out for you and for many
for the forgiveness of sins.
Do this, as often as you drink it,
in remembrance of me."

Remembering, therefore, your gracious and bountiful acts
    in Jesus Christ,
we offer these signs of your bounty:
these gifts of bread and wine,
and ourselves,
as a sacrifice of praise
as we proclaim the mystery of faith:

Christ has died; Christ is risen; Christ will come again.

Pour out your Holy Spirit on us gathered here,
and on these gifts of bread and wine,
that we may be renewed and restored to unity
with you and with all the world.
By your Spirit make us one with Christ,
one with each other,
and one in ministry to the world,
until Christ comes in final fulfillment
and we feast at his heavenly banquet.

Through your Wisdom Jesus Christ,
in the power of the Holy Spirit,
all honor and glory is yours, Holy One,
now and forever.

Amen.

RESOURCES FOR MEALS

Capon, Robert Farrar. *The Supper of the Lamb: A Culinary Reflection*. New York: Modern Library Reprints, 2002.

Goudey, June Christine. *The Feast of Our Lives: Re-imagining Communion*. Cleveland: Pilgrim Press, 2002.

Juengst, Sara Covin. *Breaking Bread: The Spiritual Significance of Food*. Louisville: Westminster John Knox Press, 1992.

Jung, Shannon. *Sharing Food: Christian Practices for Enjoyment*. Minneapolis: Fortress Press, 2006.

Kingsolver, Barbara, Steven Hopp, and Camille Kingsolver. *Animal, Vegetable, Miracle: A Year of Food Life*. New York: HarperCollins, 2007.

Procter-Smith, Marjorie. *Praying with Our Eyes Open: Engendering Feminist Liturgical Prayer*. Nashville: Abingdon Press, 1995.

TWELVE

HEALING

Come to me, all you that are weary and are carrying heavy burdens,
and I will give you rest.
Take my yoke upon you, and learn from me;
for I am gentle and humble of heart,
and you will find rest for your souls.
For my yoke is easy, and my burden is light.

—Matthew 11:28–30

THINKING ABOUT HEALING

We live in a world of hurt, and pain. All who breathe suffer, and all cry out for healing. Not only we humans suffer and cry out, but the very earth, the air, the water, the land itself also suffers and cries out for healing. The more we see that we are all part of the whole, all interconnected in life and in death, the more we seek to recover and restore that wholeness that is our birthright, as humans and as creatures of this earth. The foundational story of Christianity is the story of the wholeness of a Garden, and of its loss and our separation from the completion of the Garden, our separation from each other, and our separation from our true selves. Rituals of healing, common to all cultures and religions, seek to recover and restore that wholeness and peace that we long for in our hearts.

Feminist Healing Pathways

It is not surprising that the very earliest feminist liturgies were liturgies of healing. For women, suffering is not only our common lot as human beings but has been assigned to us as our duty and responsibility. The original creation story gives the woman the role of suffering pain in childbirth and suffering oppression at the hand of her husband. Traditional Christian interpreters have seen this story as demonstrating women's guilt for the fall and expulsion from the Garden and as justifying women's suffering of all sorts. In fact, this verse in Genesis was used to deny women any kind of painkillers during childbirth until well into the twentieth century. Women's lot, it is argued, is to suffer. And we do. Domestic violence, rape, incest, battering, sexual and domestic slavery, psychological abuse, denial of access to education, to financial resources, to political voice, to the control of our own bodies, even to food, is women's lot across the globe. It is no wonder that when women began to claim liturgical authority, liturgies of healing were the first order of business.

And from this history, a feminist practice of healing rituals has arisen. By following the feminist pathways to Wisdom's house outlined in chapter 1, we can reflect on the sources of our hurt and the resources for our healing.

The wisdom of our lives as silenced and subjugated persons tells us that we need to be healed from being defined as other, as inferior, as incomplete and incompetent. We can draw on our daily, perhaps sometimes secret, experience of God, the Holy One. We can listen to our own hearts and take pity on our suffering selves. We can begin in hope, for to engage in a healing liturgy is to engage in a practice of hope. And hope is itself a sign of healing.

The wisdom of our bodies tells us that we need to be healed from the damage done by traditional religions' rejection and fear of our bodies, bodies of women, bodies with skin that is not "white," bodies that look or act or sound different, bodies that love others like themselves. We can draw on authentic images of our bodies, images in which we recognize ourselves in our amazing beauty and uniqueness and wonder, and we can value our bodies' knowledge as holy and wise. We can create rituals simple and complex, private and communal, that celebrate and delight in the wondrous workings of our bodies, in youth and in old age, at birth and at death. We can use our bodies as part of our prayers and rituals, by anointing, moving, touching. Those of us who are temporarily able-bodied can learn from our sisters and brothers with disabilities about the experience of living with bodies that differ from the norm and how different bodies can be used in prayer and ritual.

The wisdom of our suffering and struggle tells us that we need to be healed from our encounters with evil, especially when it causes harm to our bodies by rape, incest, battering, and abuse. We need to be healed from our encounters with spiritual, theological, and psychological evil, especially when it causes harm to our spirits, our minds, and our hearts by ridicule, rejection, denial, hatred, and ignorance. We can draw on the history of resistance to suffering and oppression.

The wisdom of relationships tells us that we need to be healed from and repent of horizontal violence, the striking out at those who also suffer instead of seeing our common suffering and struggle. We can draw on connections with other women, with others who have suffered and who suffer still, celebrating and lamenting our common ground, naming and honoring our differences, claiming our mutual interconnections, dreaming, as Adrienne Rich says, of a common language.

This wisdom of our lives, bodies, struggles, and relationships also warns against potential traps that can prevent healing and even do further harm. First among these traps is the temptation to romanticize our bodies, our experiences, our relationships, or even our struggles. Unrealistic romanticizing is the enemy of honesty and truth, which are foundational for healing and wholeness. And romanticizing our suffering and our struggles fosters feelings of victimization, which can also stand in the way of wholeness. At the same time, we must resist traditional religious identification of illness, suffering, or pain with either sin or divine judgment. Pain and suffering are sometimes undeserved and sometimes a consequence of something we have done. Yet the Holy One does not seek our suffering but rather our wholeness and well-being. This too must be a basic premise of healing rituals and prayers.

Healing, Cursing, and Exorcism

It is also important to remember that healing sometimes requires surgery. Damage must be exposed to the air and the light, it must be named and the source of the pain removed. The Bible, especially the book of Psalms, is full of laments that include curses, calling down divine judgment upon the psalmist's or Israel's enemies. Ritually speaking, ritual curses and liturgical exorcisms are also healing liturgies. The curse names the evil that causes suffering; exorcism removes it, casts it out. As in the case of medical surgery, the use of curses and exorcisms must be understood to be a last ritual resort, to be employed only with the greatest care and only after other ritual treatments have failed to accomplish healing.

But if we believe that blessings are effective, especially understood as a calling out of the holiness that is already present in the object of the blessing (whether a person or a thing), then curses too must be understood as effective, in that they are a means of recognizing and calling out evil. The use of curses and exorcisms requires great spiritual maturity and deep understanding of the power of rituals and should never be undertaken lightly. But when used with care and knowledge, they can both have healing benefits.

A SPIRITUAL DISCIPLINE OF HEALING

We do well to remember that all suffering is communal and all healing is communal. As Paul observes in 1 Corinthians 12:26, "If one member suffers, all suffer together with it; if one member is honored, all rejoice together with it." A spiritual discipline of healing is based on developing attentiveness to this interconnection.

1. *Cultivate attentiveness to one's own body.* The same disciplines of bodily self-care that are suggested in chapter 5, "Body," apply here as well. In instances of bodily illness or damage, breathing practices and attention to rest and nutrition become even more important.

2. *Cultivate attentiveness to the bodies of others.* Compassion and empathy for others, and awareness of both bodily difference and bodily similarity strengthen our sense of interconnections.

3. *Cultivate attention to the physical, emotional, and spiritual needs of others.* This may be done by being attentive not only to those one encounters directly in daily life, but also to those at a distance. Such attentiveness requires careful reading of news reports and other accounts of events around the world.

4. *Cultivate attention to the needs of the nonhuman world around us.* This means giving thought to the natural environment, not only our immediate context, but our global environment as well. Small personal changes as well as national and global changes can foster healing of the natural world in which we live. At the very least, we can make every effort to reduce our harmful effects on the environment.

PATTERNS FOR HEALING

Healing liturgies and rituals are best understood as rituals undertaken in order to change something. They are motivated by our desire for wholeness, well-being, and health in all its forms. But they also recognize dissatisfaction with things the way they are at present. Whether the healing is for past hurts, ongoing illness, or present painful circumstances, there is urgency to our desire for a change for the better.

An ancient liturgical prayer form for expressing this desire for change is found throughout the Hebrew Bible, and especially in the book of Psalms. The psalms of lament generally include these elements: a declaration of harm done, a demand for restitution and restoration, and a contingent offer of praise if the conditions are changed. This basic shape provides a helpful structure for developing liturgies of lament and healing.

1. *Naming*. The healing process begins with the naming of the harm done, and the naming takes place before witnesses, including God (sometimes, under some circumstances, God may be the *only* witness). This is the point at which curses might be employed, as a form of calling out evil, and exorcism as removing it.

2. *Acknowledgement*. This is the response of the witnesses to the naming of suffering. Receiving recognition and acknowledgement of the harm done or the pain suffered is an important step in the healing process. It authenticates the reality of the pain and establishes the need for healing and restoration. It is ideal if the one(s) who caused the harm is (are) among those who witness the naming of harm done.

3. *Claiming*. The one who seeks healing is now authorized to claim the right to be restored to well-being. This is an especially important step for those who have internalized the harm and taken responsibility in place of the perpetrator(s). If the one who seeks healing is in fact in some way responsible for her own suffering, this too can be acknowledged as foundational to claiming restoration. The claim may be put in the form of a demand to the

Holy One. As is clear in many of the biblical psalms, there are times when it appears that God is in fact the responsible party rather than the judge. But in any case, the assumption of the lament form and of healing rituals and prayers is that, responsible or not, God is capable of providing relief from suffering.

4. *Praise.* Praise to God in a lament/healing liturgy is appropriately contingent: "my heart *shall* rejoice in your salvation," sings the psalmist in Psalm 13.

5. *Commitment.* Finally, it is appropriate that the witnesses commit themselves and their community to work toward bringing about the structural changes that will prevent future harm to self and others. This step should be carefully thought through so that it goes beyond symbolic ritual gestures empty of intention but makes room for concrete and specific actions that will enable healing change. The form that this portion of the liturgy takes will be determined by the nature of the harm done and by the desires of the person seeking healing.

Because healing often focuses on physical restoration and health, it is valuable to include physical elements in the liturgy. It is worth noting that prayers of lament in the ancient Near East involved performance with the whole body. Time for lament and mourning was extended; sound in the form of drums, instruments, crying aloud, or silence was part of the lament; and physical actions such as tearing one's clothing, cutting one's hair, or putting dust on one's head were also included. The mourners or petitioners might employ strategies of resistance or refusal; food, comfort, sleep might be refused. It is also worth noting that in later Christian centuries some of the same ritual practices came to be associated with beseeching God for protection from natural disasters, for success in harvest time, for peace in times of war, and for forgiveness of one's sins.

In modern times, rituals of lament and petitions for healing are often found in contexts of social protests and calls for justice. Vigils, marches, silent processions, the use of sound in chants and songs, and the use of visuals such as special dress or garment, posters, placards, or pictures are often included. One thinks, for example, of the

Black Sash movement in South Africa, the Women in Black in Israel and worldwide, and Las Locas de Plaza de Mayo in Argentina. Black Sash was originally a white women's resistance movement protesting apartheid in South Africa, in which women wearing black sashes as a sign of mourning and protest worked to bring about an end to apartheid. Black Sash continues today as an interracial human rights organization. Women in Black was started in Israel by women who dressed in black to mourn the dead of both Israelis and Palestinians and to witness for peace. The movement is now an international organization that works and witnesses for peace around the world. Las Locas de Plaza de Mayo in Argentina, also known as Las Madres de Plaza de Mayo, began as a spontaneous gathering of mothers of young men and women who had been "disappeared" by the Argentinian military regime in 1976, in which mothers wearing white scarves and bearing pictures of their missing daughters and sons gathered weekly in silence in the public square of Buenos Aires. Their silent protest and lament caught the imagination and conscience of the world. In all the examples we see the power of public lament as a witness to suffering.

In addition to considering these religious, social, and political practices of lament, we may also consider some of the social and religious practices associated with healing. These may be thought of in two categories: medicinal and purifying. Medicinal ingredients are things that have been understood to have healing properties or benefits, such as oils, foods, and touch. The use of oil as medical treatment is of ancient origins, and vegetable oils, especially olive oil, were often mixed with aromatic herbs or extracts for added benefits. Such scented oils are readily available for use in massage or bathing, but they are also simple to make. Oils can be used to anoint the body or part of the body, to prepare a healing bath, or to massage tired muscles. The medicinal use of food is also of ancient origins and is becoming better understood today. Foods that are simple, organic, and whole are the best when used in a healing ritual. Food is also associated with nurture and care, so that including food in a healing ritual can be very powerful.

Purifying ingredients are elements that have been understood to serve as cleansing agents. Water, salt, incense, candles, and fire have powerful purifying associations and can be important elements in any healing ritual or prayer. Water is cleansing, and the ritual might include washing of hands, of the affected part of the body (if there is one), or even a bathing of the whole body. Burning incense cleanses and refreshes the air and is associated with purification in many cultures. It also carries implications of blessing as well, another important aspect of healing. Candles as bearers of light in darkness suggest hope. Like incense, candles may be scented and so bless the air. They may also be a means of burning symbols or objects that are associated with the suffering being healed, both as a form of exorcism or destruction of pain, and as a purifying and blessing of the suffering. Finally, the use of objects that signify health and well-being to the one seeking healing may also be included. These might be such things as photographs, herbs or flowers, natural objects such as shells, stones, feathers, or seeds, items of clothing, special foods, and the like.

PRAYERS FOR HEALING

A Healing Liturgy

(The individual seeking healing chooses objects that represent health and well-being. These objects are placed in the center of the room or gathering space. The person seeking healing gathers together with those who have been invited to participate around this center. One person has been designated by the one seeking healing as the guide for this liturgy.)

GUIDE: We gather for (*Name*), for *her* well-being, for *her* peace, for *her* restoration, saying (singing), Holy One, hear us.

Holy One, hear us.

GUIDE: We gather for (*Name*), in *her* presence, in your presence, to bear witness to *her* suffering.

Holy One, hear us.

GUIDE: (*Name*), name your suffering in our presence and in the presence of the Holy One.

(Here the one seeking healing names her/his suffering, illness, or pain.)

Holy One, hear us.

GUIDE: (*Name*) name the healing you seek, in our presence and in the presence of the Holy One.

(Here the one seeking healing names her/his need.)

Holy One, hear us.

GUIDE: Holy One, we beg you to see this suffering to which we all bear witness.

We beg you to bring the healing (*Name*) requests and to which we all bear witness.

We promise to remember you and give you thanks.

We promise to work to end suffering where we can and
when we can,

and to call on you for strength and courage and help.

Holy One, hear us.

*(Here the Guide and others as requested by the one seeking healing use
oil, incense, smoke, water, or other healing practice requested by the one
seeking healing.)*

GUIDE: (*Name*), what do you ask of us, in the presence of
the Holy One?

*(Here the one seeking healing may request any help needed, such as
prayers, meal preparation, babysitting, transportation, house cleaning or
grocery shopping, or any other appropriate assistance. Those present make
any appropriate commitments in response to these requests.)*

GUIDE: We hear your needs, we offer our assistance, we give
thanks to the Holy One for the gift of your life, we seek your
well-being and the well-being of all.

(Here, those present may share in food and companionship as desired.)

A MEAL PRAYER OF BITTERNESS[17]

*(A mourning meal to be observed in times of great suffering and loss, but
in hope of restoration. Let there be two breads and two cups. Let one
bread be tasteless, stale. Let the other be sweet, perhaps made with raisins
or other dried fruit. Let one cup be filled with bitter wine, or vinegar, or
salt water. Let the second cup be filled with sweet wine or fruit juice. Let
the participants bring nonmusical noisemakers: rattles, drums, ratchets,
and the like, to wake up God.)*

May God hear our cry.

May God read the signs of our hearts.

Bring your complaints before God.

We bring our sorrows and accusations.

O God, you have promised to be with us, but you have hidden your face;
you have called and claimed us as your own,
but you have let our enemies triumph over us.

Where were you, O God, when we needed you?
(Sound noisemakers)

When Jephtha murdered his daughter in payment to you,
where were you?

Where were you, O God, when we needed you?
(Sound noisemakers)

When the Levite's concubine was raped and murdered and
dismembered,
where were you?

Where were you, O God, when we needed you?
(Sound noisemakers)

When Tamar was raped by her brother,
where were you?

Where were you, O God, when we needed you?
(Sound noisemakers)

(Here let members of the assembly name their complaints against God, in direct address to God. To each complaint, let all respond:)

Where were you, O God, when we needed you?
(Sound noisemakers)

(After the final complaint, a leader says:)

Together with the suffering and the oppressed,
the raped and the betrayed,
the battered and the murdered, we cry:

**Because of you we are being killed all day long,
and accounted as sheep for the slaughter.
Rouse yourself! Why do you sleep, O God?**
(Sound noisemakers)

Jesus too knew betrayal and abandonment.
On the night he was betrayed by his friends and abandoned
    to suffering and death,
Jesus took the bread of betrayal, prayed to you, and gave it
    to them, saying:
"Take, eat; this is my body. Whenever you do this, remember
    me."
Then he took the cup of bitterness, prayed to you, and
    shared it with them, saying:
"Drink this, all of you. This is my blood, poured out.
Whenever you do this, remember me."

In remembrance of all the forgotten, abandoned, and neg-
    lected ones,
we share this bread of betrayal and cup of bitterness.
All those you have forgotten, we remember in this bread
    and this cup.

(Here let the bread of affliction be shared. Let the cup of bitterness be passed around.)

We remember too that in raising Jesus from the dead you
    refused his death.
Refuse our suffering and death
and the suffering of all who are now abandoned by you.

Why do you hide your face?
Why do you forget our affliction and oppression?
(Sound noisemakers)

Awake, O God, and remember us.
Send us your Spirit.
Come to our help and to the help of all who suffer and call
    on you.

Rise up, come to our help.
Save us for the sake of your steadfast love.
Amen.

(In hope, now share the sweet bread and wine.)

RESOURCES FOR HEALING

Billman, Kathleen, and Daniel Migliore. *Rachel's Cry: Prayer of Lament and Rebirth of Hope*. Cleveland: United Church Press, 1999.

Circles of Healing: A Support Group Curriculum for Abused Christian Women. Seattle: FaithTrust Institute, 2003.

Henderson, Frank J. *Liturgies of Lament*. Chicago: Liturgy Training Publications, 1994.

Iser, Alison, Michelle Lifton, Lisa Gelber, Condy Enger, Irit Eliav, and Leigh Nachman Hofheimer, eds. *A Journey Toward Freedom: A Haggadah for Women Who Have Experienced Domestic Violence*. Seattle: FaithTrust Institute, 2003.

Landesman, Toby. *You Are Not Alone: Solace and Inspiration for Domestic Violence Survivors Based on Jewish Wisdom*. Seattle: FaithTrust Institute, 2004.

Weems, Ann. *Psalms of Lament*. Louisville: Westminster John Knox Press, 1995.

Zimmerman, Mari West. *Take and Make Holy: Honoring the Sacred in the Healing Journey of Abuse Survivors*. Chicago: Liturgy Training Publications, 1995.

NOTES

1. See Nelle Morton, *The Journey Is Home* (Boston: Beacon Press, 1985). See also "Nelle Morton: Hearing to Speech," in *The Christian Century* (February 7–14, 1990); and "Nelle Morton: Journeying Home," in *The Christian Century* (August 26–September 2, 1987).

2. Anne Cameron, *Daughters of Copper Woman* (Vancouver: Press Gang Press, 1981), 58.

3. Ntozake Shange, *For Colored Girls Who Have Considered Suicide When the Rainbow Is Enuf* (New York: Macmillan, 1977), 63.

4. Tom F. Driver, *Liberating Rites: Understanding the Transformative Power of Ritual* (Boulder, Colo.: Westview Press, 1998), 93.

5. Theodore Jennings Jr. , "On Ritual Knowledge," in *Readings in Ritual Studies,* ed. Ronald L. Grimes (Upper Saddle River, N.J.: Prentice-Hall, 1995), 324–34.

6. Filipe Tohi, "Christ the Anchor," in *Christ for All People: Celebrating a World of Christian Art,* ed. Ron O'Grady (Maryknoll, N.Y.: Orbis Press, 2001. Used by permission.

7. Yi-Fu Tuan, *Topophilia: A Study of Environmental Perception, Attitude, and Values* (New York: Prentice-Hall, 1974), 28.

8. Cameron, *Daughters of Copper Woman,* 58.

9. Jonathan Z. Smith, *To Take Place: Toward Theory in Ritual* (Chicago: University of Chicago, 1987), 103.

10. Marge Piercy, "The Sabbath of Mutual Respect," *The Moon Is Always Female* (New York: A. Knopf, 1980), 104ff.

11. Esther M. Broner, *A Weave of Women* (Bloomington: Indiana University Press, 1985), 256.

12. Adapted from the Hymn of Christ, The Acts of John, fourth century C.E.

13. *The United Methodist Hymnal* (Nashville: United Methodist Publishing House, 1989).

14. *The Presbyterian Hymnal: Hymns, Psalms, and Spiritual Songs* (Westminster John Knox Press, 1990).

15. *Renewing Worship Volume 5: New Hymns and Songs* (Augsburg/ Fortress, 2003 Lutheran trial hymnal).

16. *New Century Hymnal* (Cleveland: Pilgrim Press, 1995).

17. Text adapted from Marjorie Procter-Smith, *Praying with Our Eyes Open: Engendering Feminist Liturgical Prayer* (Nashville: Abingdon Press, 1995). Adapted by permission.